Minimalist Budget:

30 Days to Minimalism! Discover Amazing Benefits and Powerful Strategies of Minimalist Budgeting to Save Money, Pay Off Debt, Avoid Emotional Spending, Build Discipline, Declutter!

© **Copyright by Tony Bennis 2019 - All rights reserved.**

The content contained within this book may not be reproduced, duplicated or transmitted without direct written permission from the author or the publisher.

Under no circumstances will any blame or legal responsibility be held against the publisher, or author, for any damages, reparation, or monetary loss due to the information contained within this book. Either directly or indirectly.

Legal Notice:

This book is copyright protected. This book is only for personal use. You cannot amend, distribute, sell, use, quote or paraphrase any part, or the content within this book, without the consent of the author or publisher.

Disclaimer Notice:

Please note the information contained within this document is for educational and entertainment purposes only. All effort has been executed to present accurate, up to date, and reliable, complete information. No warranties of any kind are declared or implied. Readers acknowledge that the author is not engaging in the rendering of legal, financial, medical or professional advice. The content within this book has been derived from various sources. Please consult a licensed professional before attempting any techniques outlined in this book.

By reading this document, the reader agrees that under no circumstances is the author responsible for any losses, direct or indirect, which are incurred as a result of the use of information contained within this document, including, but not limited to, — errors, omissions, or inaccuracies.

Table of Contents

Introduction..6

Chapter 1: What Is a Minimalist Budget?....7

Chapter 2: Benefits of Minimalism.............13

Chapter 3: Why Minimalism Doesn't Work for Some People..29

Chapter 4: How to Create a Minimalist Budget...38

Chapter 5: Myths of Minimalist Budgeting..50

Chapter 6: Some Basic Financial Principles...53

Chapter 7: Debt...59

Chapter 8: Tips on Saving Money as a Minimalist..72

Chapter 9: How to Build Discipline............76

Chapter 10: Tips on Becoming a Minimalist..90

Chapter 11: Decluttering..........................102

Chapter 12: Is Minimalism Boring?..........108

Chapter 13: Handling Relationships with Non-Minimalists.......................................117

Chapter 14: 30 Days to Minimalism—A Simple Guide...124

Conclusion..145
References...146

Introduction

Most of us have to hustle to cover our expenses and needs. After we have been paid for a job well done, we all want to be able to use the money in such a way that it meets all our needs (and then some) without being completely depleted. So, we reevaluate our spending, create budgets, and try several strategies in a bid to extend the lifespan of our finances and put an end to the paycheck to paycheck living. All that is good and will be discussed in this book. But, without a solid plan, all our resolutions are destined to go up in smoke, whether or not they are for the new year or mid year.

There have been many misconceptions and false information on the subject of minimalist budgets and minimalism in general. The book, ***Minimalist Budget: A Practical Guide to Managing a Minimalist Life***, was written to correct this erroneous perception about what a minimalist budget entails. This book will not only help you effectively manage your finances, it will also reveal to you the many other benefits of a minimalist lifestyle, which include a much happier life.

Abandon all you have learned about minimalism and enter the pages of this book with a curious, critical, and open mind. Be willing to make the necessary lifestyle changes. You'll be glad you did.

Chapter 1: What Is a Minimalist Budget?

The analytics company Gallup conducted a survey in 2013 to determine how many Americans write, in detail, a budget for their personal finances (Jacobe, 2013). The result exposed that less than one in every three Americans had a comprehensive budget for their household finances. This means, if you are an American, there is every possibility that you spend your earnings without the plan or strategy that a budget provides. Now you might be thinking, *I'm not from the U.S., and I do not even live in the country.* Unfortunately, the result of the poll performed by Gallup is one shared by most people in many countries of the world. That same year, another financial poll was done in Canada ("Household"). It discovered that the average Canadian family spent, on things like food, shelter and transportation, a total of 62.14% of their earnings. This does not include expenses on education, clothing, furniture, healthcare, alcohol, gambling, and so on.

Clearly, the struggle to control the many outlets that empty our bank accounts is one shared by the majority of us. We can agree that there is a need for a budget plan that works. That said, I present to you the minimalist budget.

The minimalist budget is one that does away with the complexities that have become synonymous with many traditional budgeting plans. Basically, your expenses should be channeled towards only the very essentials of your daily life. So, instead of fantasizing about a Gucci bag on your shoulder, your primary concern would have to things like rent, insurance, groceries, and the like. Minimalist budgeting keeps your focus on the future, but away from the trivial and ephemeral. It also encourages you to own only necessities and weed out the things you have no use for. This is because we, as human beings in general, devote a lot of our time, money, physical energy, and mental energy to maintaining our properties. As such, it only follows that the more of such properties you own, the time, energy, and money you would expend.

Before we dive further into the minimalist budget, let us understand what is meant by minimalism and how it started.

The Origin and Concept of Minimalism

Determining the exact moment in time that the idea of minimalism was born can be problematic. This is because the further you walk down the shifting sands of time, the more examples of minimalist ideologies you find. They can be seen in religion, with different groups upholding a sometimes extremely simplistic lifestyle. Adherents to such beliefs subsist with the bare minimum and choose poverty over any semblance of luxury or comfort. Figures like Jesus, Mohammed, Gandhi, and Confucius were all advocates for a life of very little. This they did for the reward of spiritual enlightenment. Generally speaking, those who lived on few possessions by reason of their religious faith were of the belief that earthly belongings, especially in large numbers, represented a detour on their journey of spiritual progress. So they unburdened themselves and went about simply. There are still many who choose minimalism for religious purposes.

But the way in which minimalism has caught on in modern times may be thanks to minimalist art, which began something of a movement after the Second World War. It was, arguably, at its most intense stage in the early 70s. In fact, decluttering and a simplistic lifestyle had nothing to do with the term *minimalism* when it was first in use. It took off in the music world, as several composers thought it better to strip their pieces to only a few instruments. Some early minimalist music composers include Michael Nyman, Tom Johnson, Philip Glass, Steve Reich, and La Monte Young. In the words of Tom Nyman, "The idea of minimalism...includes, by definition, any music that works with limited or minimal materials" (Johnson, 1989). This would later extend beyond music, as painters, photographers, architects and other designers would climb aboard the minimalist train.

Abstract expressionism, a style of painting that was the most popular form at the time, was pushed aside in favor of more geometric and less flamboyant or dramatic styles. Instead of drawing people to the emotional meaning or biography associated with their art (devices used in abstract expressionism), they placed the focus on the inartistic materials employed and simple brush strokes used to create coordinated and sleek works.

Over time, the ideology of using only the bare minimum slowly filtered into households. Instead of enjoying simplistic music and other forms of art, people started to incorporate the philosophy of minimalism into their lifestyle. And with decluttering guru Marie Kondo now enjoying worldwide fame for teaching people to do away with stuff in their homes because such stuff adds nothing to the level of their happiness, lifestyle minimalism is one trend that, apparently, has come to stay.

Minimalism is not about living in a bare house and relishing the echoes as a financial accomplishment. It is not about working for peanuts and feeding on grains of sand. Ridiculous and funny as these images might seem, there are many people whose definition of a minimalist lifestyle would bear close similarity to them. While many other myths about minimalism and the minimalist budget will be discussed in a later chapter, it must be stressed here that the only rule about the concept of minimalism that is set in stone is that one should live on only the things they need. From the clothes hanging in your wardrobe, the food in your refrigerator, and the furniture in your home, each item must have a clearly defined purpose in relationship with your needs.

With the rate at which more and more people continue to spend their way into the quicksand of debt, it is no surprise that the minimalist lifestyle is more appealing today than ever before. There is also a correlation between happiness and minimalism. In a study carried out by Northwestern University, it was proven in a roundabout way that there is some fact to the old saying: money cannot buy happiness. The research revealed a higher risk of depression and antisocial tendencies for those individuals who placed a premium on their stuff, their social standing, and riches, rather than relationships and happiness (Bodenhausen et al., 2012). True happiness does not come about by the accumulation of material possessions. There are several ways to truly enjoy life without having to wait on the praises of strangers as they view you on Instagram posing with a $500 watch. That kind of living instills in you the habit of self-absorption. And people who choose that path may hold the philosophy, later on, that life is without meaning.

Well, life can be meaningful. Since the quality of our mental and emotional health is not separate from the level of our materialism, applying the minimalist philosophy to your personal finances may just be what you need to discover joy and fulfilment.

Chapter 2: Benefits of Minimalism

Minimalism is beneficial in a lot of ways; it is almost clichéd from many discussions. However, there are many different and important aspects of our lives in which minimalism can play a beneficial role. These aspects are inclusive but not limited to, the following:

- Finance
- Health
- Psychology
- Environment

To better understand how minimalism is of benefit to us in these aspects mentioned above, we will individually discuss them.

The Financial Benefits of Minimalism

The financial benefits of minimalism are open to those who are minimalists by practice—people who have freed themselves of distractions to embrace the opportunities which come their way. Contrary to popular stereotypes, minimalism doesn't imply that you have to become strung up and miserly with your money. No. If anything, that is in no way part of its ideas or concepts. Instead, the concept of minimalism mandates that money is spent on things that are worth the trouble.

That said, let's delve right into the benefits minimalism can have on your finances.

1. Minimalism gives you a paradigm shift.

A paradigm shift refers to any change in perspective from one specific belief to another one, prompted by new discoveries which reveal irregularities in the present model. When simplified further, it means changing the mindset.

Practicing minimalism gives you a paradigm shift which transforms your senses from that of a *consumer* to one of an *investor*. That shift completely recharacterizes the way you look at resources. How long will they last? How long will the benefits last? What constitutes satisfaction and fulfillment? Who benefits from such resources? Will there be collateral damage from the use of this resource? What impact(s) will result? When you view the world as an investor, you give careful thought to factors you would otherwise not consider when making financial decisions. In this vein, you are more likely to choose to invest your money over purchasing liabilities which promise short-term benefits.

As a minimalist, you learn to make the most of less, and thrive on little expenditure. This marks the beginning of your ability to perceive as an investor. And although it may not be so obvious that you would quickly notice, the state of your finances will gradually improve. Let's take some examples of how this may occur.

Rather than spending your money on mindless, binge shopping, you would opt to save, and when you choose to spend, you would only buy things when they are an absolute necessity. Another mindset change would occur in the sense of preferring frugality over extravagance. But your sense of frugality will not be limited to spending money alone, you will also use your time prudently, by letting go of activities which cost you more than they benefit you. By so doing, you will be able to invest your time on more important and worthwhile things. And as the popular maxim states, "time is money."

2. Minimalism helps improve your plans for retirement.

Sometimes the reason we spend money without thinking is that we have both poor motivations and give no thought to the future. Let's see how this works. First, we sometimes spend money on impulse in which nothing other than our immediate satisfaction drives our actions. On the other hand, when little to no thought is given to the future, we tend to live for the moment alone. Strange how we forget every day has a tomorrow. Pairing both, the prospect of a retirement plan in the context of such behaviors is as impossible as it is laughable.

But how does minimalism work in this regard? Simple. When you opt to live a life of less, you tend to increase your chances of saving and investing, all which can be tunneled into getting yourself a healthy retirement. In turn, getting your retirement all planned out and funded will reduce the mental and emotional stress associated with any anxiety you may have about the future. What's more, you could also trigger the prospect of early retirement by the singular act of practicing minimalism.

3. Minimalism helps you save on expenditure.

The ideology behind minimalism is getting more for less, and this concept can go a great way in your expenditure. Purchasing things has come to be one of the many inevitabilities of human existence, so it would be a big aid if we somehow managed to get more value at a lower price. And believe you me, this is no promo. Minimalism is the word.

As one who practices minimalism, you will trim your amount of belongings. This means less clutter and less space required to store your stuff. As such, when renting, leasing, or buying a property, you can opt for a moderate-sized space and would not have to pay through your nose to secure it. Your property will be able to store your stuff without extensions which cost more money while remaining comfy and nice. This is but a brief description of how you can harness more from less. If you aren't minimalist yet and have much clutter, you can compare how minimalism fares to extravagance by decluttering and relocating to a smaller apartment. You would be surprised how much you can save on rent, utilities or mortgage without being uncomfortable or upsetting your lifestyle.

The Environmental Benefits of Minimalism

The benefits that minimalism yields also affect the environment in a positive way. And although it doesn't prevent climate change in an instant or clear the oceans and seas of plastic pollution, it does help save the planet one person at a time. Let's see how minimalism works in this regard.

1. Minimalism is an eco-friendly practice.

Perhaps we are too focused on how to save the planet by all means that we miss out on one of the major factors destroying the earth—excesses. And minimalism is the only way out because if everyone had just enough stuff to live on, our impact on the planet would be drastically reduced. This can be achieved if we all stay mindful of what we spend our money on, what we consume and how much we produce. If all these are properly regulated, we will reduce the speed at which the resources on the planet suffer exhaustion.

For instance, consider the amount of packaging that goes into your purchases as well as that of other people. Stores would typically hand you your purchases in bags (plastic, paper, cloth, etc. depending on your purchases). Online stores, on the other hand, usually box your orders or use other packing materials like bubble wrap and nylon. That aside, the goods come covered in plastic themselves. And if you purchase clothes, they come with tags. Just these simple factors affect the environment in more ways than they seem. So, it turns out saving the environment relies more on us people being minimalist in our dealings rather than rallying to save the planet on Earth Day while polluting it still.

As a minimalist, instead of opting to buy a large amount of short-term stuff, you buy quality items that are durable and fewer of them. By so doing, you will be contributing less waste to the environment in the long run, which would otherwise not be the case if you had chosen to buy short-term products.

2. Minimalism helps regulate consumerism.

Consumerism is a theory in economics which opines that an increment in consumer consumption holds beneficial returns for the economy of a country for a long period. The concepts behind consumerism contribute immensely to the slow death of the planet and climate change. Reports show that an estimate of 60% of all emissions of greenhouse gases around the world stems from consumerism. How did this come to be? With the advent of online trading came the trend of people buying goods from different regions of the world. Owing to the difference in geographical location, the goods have to be transported to the buyer. The farther the buyer is from the seller, the more diverse the modes of transportation used to forward the goods. Those various, accumulated trips result in accumulated carbon emissions from the vehicles that carry your next Prime order and increased consumption of fossil fuels to fuel them on their journeys. Every increase in sales for a company like Amazon or Alibaba means an increase in climate-changing pollution.

Another aspect of consumerism which greatly hurts the environment is fashion. The rapid evolution of fashion trends results in lots of clothes being sold every day of the week. Such consumption then results in higher demand for clothing materials and increased levels of waste. The demand for clothing materials means using up more resources such as water, plants like cotton, and animals like sheep, among others. On the other hand, waste comes in the form of pollutants found in areas where they shouldn't be on account of improper disposal, causing harm to animals and plants. When summed up, the fashion and textile industries constitute a strain on the environment by using up valuable energy, polluting the environment, and exhausting the planet's resources. The entire process, ranging from sourcing for raw materials to production to eventual sales, impacts the environment negatively.

Studies show that two decades before now, humans used 400 percent less clothing materials than they currently do. Further reports went on to state that people consume around 80 billion clothing materials every year, owing to the high demands of the fashion market and the growth of evolving trends ("The True Cost"). How then does minimalism fit in here? When minimalism is practiced, consumerism will greatly reduced. If only people downsized their stuff now and then and bought what was needed as a replacement for older stuff, the impact of consumerism on the environment could be reversed.

The Psychological Benefits of Minimalism

The beneficial effects of minimalism on a psychological level cannot be overstated. Minimalism is not limited to financial and environmental benefits alone and has been grossly understated. Let's take a look at how minimalism is beneficial on a psychological level.

1. Minimalism reduces stress.

Stress is one of the may psychological weights we humans endure in our lifetimes. It comes from many different sources and chokes us up until we shrink and retreat into our shells—becoming shadows of ourselves, or the worst versions yet.

How does minimalism help out in this regard? First, we must recognize that sometimes the stress which weighs us down is caused by environmental factors. If your environment—your living space or workspace—is choked with clutter, chances are it might get to you soon enough. The reason is that the brain goes into overdrive when it is unable to process clutter. And neither our brains nor our bodies are designed to operate in a state of constant overdrive. Eventually, something is going to shut down.

Another environmental factor is competition. The prospect of competing with others separates your self-worth, what you are, to what you can be. Competition turns your self-worth into a commodity you want to have by all means, forgetting that it's a part of you. You end up stressed out from reaching for something that was never gone in a bid to prove a point.

The same applies to physical clutter. How much clutter takes the form of memorabilia you can't seem to do away with? And how much of that memorabilia is associated with memories you don't want to remember anyway? Practicing minimalism helps you get rid of all these clutters. You can rid yourself of any physical clutter which causes negative emotions, as well as rid yourself of the mental stress of competition. And although this may not exactly rid you of all the stress you will ever feel, you would at least have dealt with stressors that you have control over. This puts you in a prime position to deal with other forms of stress more effectively.

2. Minimalism offers you a sense of happiness.

Indeed happiness is not a measure of material wealth. So regardless of how much stuff you have, if you are unhappy, that is what you are—unhappy. The ideology that happiness is tied to how much you earn or how much stuff you have is false. No correlation whatsoever exists between financial or material wealth and happiness. As such, tying your unhappiness to your lack of wealth is rather silly. The most you can get with such a mentality is a constant struggle to earn more, wishing that by some means you might encounter happiness in your search for wealth, or at least your wealth can afford it.

First of all, it's imperative you understand that happiness isn't a commodity that is sold to the highest bidder. No. If anything, it should be your return on investment (ROI) rather than something you pursue. That said, striving to get the wealth to "afford" happiness would only put you at risk of losing out on your present happiness. Thus, the pursuit of wealth for happiness is nothing but a never-ending cycle of failure. You don't want to get entwined in that.

How then does minimalism fit into the picture? As a minimalist, you learn to prioritize the important stuff over the frivolous. By so doing, you understand that true, lasting happiness stems from experiences and memories you can have with people instead of the frivolities that property or wealth can offer.

3. Minimalism brings clarity.

In a chaotic world like ours, filled with so much noise, only the night brings about some measure of quiet. It's hard to maintain clarity of mind. In as much as the bar for clarity is already set high, another obstacle in our path stems from the possessions we keep. As much as we give no thought to the effect of our physical goods on our psychology, can't deny the fact that such a connection does exist.

Research carried out on the relationship between physical properties and mental health reveals that our peace of mind and mental clarity is greatly affected each time we declutter our space. Since one of the concepts of minimalism involves downsizing to improve one's life, it's easy to see how minimalism comes into play here. Let's see how it works by taking a trip down memory lane.

Do you recall the last time you carved out time to browse through all your stuff and take out the things you no longer use? Or the last time you did the most downsizing and cleaned out a pile of clutter you had been avoiding for a while? Forget how long ago the memory was made. Focus on the feeling that swept through you after completing either of these tasks. Do you remember it? If it was anything like relief or satisfaction, then we are on the right path. Sometimes, before you did these tasks, you procrastinated and postponed a lot, so much that it began to choke you and inflict you with anxiety and stress. The very thought of the overhanging work at any point in your day just served to ruin your mood and cause anxiety. But the moment you took the time to attend to them, you felt better. Clearing them out brought you a sense of calm and clarity you hadn't experienced in a while.

Practicing minimalism ensures you maintain your sense of clarity and keep anxiety at bay by cutting down on your stuff, clearing out what you no longer use or need.

The Health Benefits of Minimalism

Minimalism also holds some benefits on the physical health front. Let's see how.

1. Minimalism improves your overall wellbeing.

The thought of simplicity and downsizing affecting your physical health may sound strange, but it is true. A change in perspective is all that is needed to see how true it is. For instance, consider how much better you would feel if you browsed through your schedule(s) and scrapped the things you find unhelpful and unimportant.

Sometimes, the problem with us is that we are so committed to our schedules, we have no time to live and be ourselves truly. If you take the time out to consider why you didn't stop at some point to catch your breath and just be yourself, the answer is usually not more than your fears. You are afraid you would disappoint someone. You are afraid to be seen as anything but hardworking and diligent. You are afraid of failing others and yourself. Because of these fears and more, you revert to overloading your schedule, making no time for breaks. Eventually, you begin to fall ill from stress, overwork, and malnourishment.

It would be a different tale had you made out the

time to take a break, breathe, and simply exist, being present in the moment without an agenda or expectation. You would have seen the loophole in your plans, trumped your fears, noticed your slipping health, and cared for yourself better. The concept of cutting down through minimalism can be put to use in many different ways without regard to what is being downsized, possessions, commitments, or schedule. You would be surprised how much your health will improve by practicing minimalism.

2. Minimalism helps you make healthier choices.

Every other day of the week, we are faced with decision making in which we are presented with different options that affect the outcome of events. But as much as making a choice seems to be a constant part of our lives, it's a shame we don't all make better choices. Why is this so? Perspectives. Everyone has had to make a choice viewed from various perspectives, accounting for why they all made the choices that best suited their point of views. However, seeing as there are chances of making wrong and bad choices, what can be done to improve the chances of making better, healthier choices? Minimalism. That's right.

As was earlier mentioned, minimalism brings about a paradigm shift. You will be able to make healthy choices if your duty to your schedules is lessened as well as your level of clutter. And as both tasks reduce stress and anxiety, and improve your perception of the important things, your perception will become sharper, and your chances of making the wrong choices will dwindle. For instance, when you clear your schedules of irrelevant tasks and focus on the important things, you will have the time to do the things you long for like exercising, taking a vacation, etc. When you aren't trying to be, do, and acquire *everything*, your few, simple values will be obvious, and you will make decisions around them. This way, you improve your health while reducing your tendency to make wrong, unhealthy choices.

3. Minimalism improves self-esteem.

As much as self-esteem is a thing of the mind, it cannot be understated the impact it has on our lives and the way we perceive things.

Low self-esteem typically sends you into a tailspin of wanting to get the clothes in fashion and the fanciest luxuries, among other frivolities. However, your desire to have all this stuff is not from your need of it, but the desire to feed your poor judgment of self. You hope that somehow they will make you feel good about yourself, or make others view you differently.

However, imagine how less choked up you would be if you didn't need frivolities to feel great about yourself or get validation from others. Practicing minimalism makes you feel good about yourself without having to be extreme in your doings. You will end up feeling better about owning less than you would with all the possessions through which you sought validation.

Chapter 3: Why Minimalism Doesn't Work for Some People

If you try to discuss the topic of minimalism with some people, not everyone of them will have nice things to say about it. Your approach to minimalism is largely influenced by your experience. And your approach will be determined by what knowledge you have gained on the subject. For example, if all you understand about minimalism is that you must rid yourself of 90% of all you possess, quit your job and move to a less than popular (or safe) location, then your minimalist story may share a regrettable similarity with those who have also failed at it.

Here is a list of some crucial reasons why you might fail and give up on minimalism.

1. **You don't forgive yourself when you fall short:** Habits are not the easiest things to change. It is especially difficult when you are turning from a lifestyle of pleasure-seeking and whim-chasing to one of modesty and simplicity. It takes a lot of discipline and resolve to commit to such a lifestyle, but no amount of lecturing and reading of books on self-control will guarantee that you never slip

up. These lapses in your judgment are sure to happen. The fact that you can identify them when they happen is a sign of progress. Don't berate yourself over this and don't belittle whatever you have achieved in your minimalist adventure. Maybe you made an online purchase of something you don't need. Take note and be determined to not find yourself in such a situation next time. Who knows, it just might happen again. But your choice of minimalism should not harm your self-esteem or make you depressed. Walk straight out of the pity party, chin up, and smile. Practice, they say, precedes perfection. Change never happens at the snap of a finger. Acknowledge your little breakthroughs and keep moving.

2. **You go all in when you should start small**: Please don't do this. There is no denying the allure of those minimalist houses on Pinterest. Of course you want to feel the same level of freedom. But here is a question: how do you get to the end of a journey without covering the distance between your starting and ending points? Again, life is not a magic carpet ride, and those little steps matter. Don't start your first day as a minimalist by throwing out most of what you own. Go easy on yourself. Instead, you could focus on decluttering your wardrobe. Even then, take baby steps. There is no point discouraging yourself from ever moving

forward with minimalism by making all the toughest decisions in your first week. The process of minimalism is as emotional as it is psychological. Ease your way into it and let the concept of simple living grow on you.

3. **Your kind of minimalism is not unique to your lifestyle**: This happens much more than it should. You might admire a certain minimalist so much that you use the same methods they do without tailoring minimalism to your unique lifestyle. Your minimalist idol may not have as hectic a life as you do or cater to as many children. They might be married while you are single. They might be seven figure earners and self-employed while you get paid five figures for your yearly income. All that is really set in stone with minimalism is that less is more. Do not break your back in an attempt to live up to the standard of your favorite minimalist. It is unnecessary and unproductive. If there is anything you can change without affecting the quality of your life or the lives of those who depend on you, then do so. But then you should recognize the variables which constitute your life and pattern your method of minimalism to fit it. Maybe your minimalist idol does not write down "children's school fees" when they do their budgeting. But if you have kids, then it is something you must make provisions for. The only necessary similarity that must exist

between your brand of minimalism and those of people whom you admire or respect is that you should purchase, use, and have in your house only those things you need.

4. **You think a minimalist lifestyle is all about near-empty white houses**: This is one instance where knowledge, indeed, is power. There is the misguided notion harbored by certain people that those curated, all-white homes with little more than three or four pieces of furniture are the ideal living spaces for true minimalists. There are some problems with this perception. For one, such homes are not, exactly, cheap to come by. Many of the pictures you see are products of studio lighting and hours of editing. Some of the furniture you see in those pictures are not the most affordable in the market, which defeats the entire purpose of minimalism. Another problem is how excruciatingly hard it is to maintain your house in such a way. If you can get your house to look as sparse and pristine as the ones on social media, then what about your kids who love to jump on the sofa or your friends who visit your home on Fridays? It is unrealistic to presume you can keep your house looking fantastically minimalist. It is alright to have a messy home. Just relax and clean it up. It doesn't mean you have broken a commandment in the law of minimalism. It only means you are a human being living in

the real world. And that's alright. It's a lot more fun.

5. **You feel overwhelmed by the amount of work to be done**: You look around your home and wonder how much time it would take to completely declutter it. Then you consider your job and other obligations, and come to the decision that minimalism just isn't for you. But, as we have already discussed, you can always tailor your minimalist approach to fit your lifestyle and schedule. If it will be impossible for you to declutter every single day of the week, then you can choose to do so only on select days. This could be Saturdays or any other day(s) you feel best suits you. Also, go as slowly as you want. Don't think you have to declutter every section in each room in just one day. Even with small houses, the mere thought of doing so can make one feel discouraged. What does it matter to anyone if it takes you three days to organize your wardrobe and two weeks to deal with your bedroom? The thing of importance is that you are getting it done, and not many people can make the same claim. As well known as the concept of minimalism is, there are more non-minimalists in the world than there are minimalists. So, if you even decide to give it a go, then that's a win in itself.

6. **You can't imagine giving up your lifestyle of buying your wants:** You've been a creature of pleasure for such a long time that you shudder at the thought of placing a limit on yourself. You can't imagine trying it out, let alone sustaining it for any length of time. You're the kind of person who walks into a clothes store to buy one shirt, but leaves with two bags full of them. Does it matter to you that the happiness you derive from such a life is not lasting? How about the issue of your finances having so many holes, you might as well be jobless? If it bothers you that you're struggling to stay afloat in a sea of debt or that you are standing dangerously close to the cliff's edge and are about to lose control of your personal finances, then this should be all the push you need to try minimalism. For some, it is simply to enjoy the feeling of reclaiming control of their lives. Most of our choices are made for us by advertising agencies, government policies, pressure from friends and family, and societal demands. How liberating it must feel to do what is right for you regardless of what those four factors have to say.

7. **Your spouse, partner, kids, and others do not want to be minimalists**: That you have chosen to take this step does not mean everyone will applaud you. It is just like every other decision you've ever made. You will encounter those who will offer their support

and those who will take the mantle of being your critics. The choice to be a minimalist tends to attract more criticism than other decisions. This is because it not only affects your life, but has a way of filtering into what is habitual and routine for those around you. Do not expect them to understand once you spell out the reason behind your stand or how it would be of benefit to those close to you. The way to go about this is to not try to impose your minimalist choices and ideologies on them. Simply restrict your decluttering and other activities to your own space. If there are certain things you have to purchase for them, then do it the way they would prefer. Let them see, from your own practice and in the improvement of your life, the advantages of going minimalist. If they never come around, that's fine. It doesn't make them bad people. But, should they seek your help with becoming a minimalist, be ready to offer all the assistance you can.

8. **What if you discard something today, but end up needing it tomorrow?**: Or, what if you part with a certain item, only to find that you were more attached to it than you realized? There is a chance, although very slim, that this might happen. But, this often occurs with people who are so engulfed in the euphoria of joining "team minimalist," that they pay little mind to the gravity of the choices they are making. Deciding to let

certain items in your house go or stay is truly serious business. It should not be done feverishly or irrationally. Be calm when you make these choices. Deliberate on the issue carefully in your mind. You will find, when you do, that you have no regrets whatsoever about the things you discard.

Here's a little exercise you could try. If, for example, you are decluttering your wardrobe, have all your clothes in three piles. The first pile should be those clothes you frequently wear and would like to keep. The next pile of clothes are those you'll throw in the thrash. Finally, have a pile for the clothes you will give to charity organizations or send as gifts to close friends or family members. When you have these three piles of clothes ready, continue to reevaluate them for about an hour before concluding. In so doing, you can be sure of your choices.

9. **You think minimalism is a cure-all**: There are certain aspects of your life you should not expect a simple lifestyle change to fix. Some people choose minimalism because they think it will make them more creative or less anxious. While these two are some of the possible benefits of living as a minimalist, it is not not advisable that you depend entirely on it. Don't choose to be a minimalist because you feel it will bring someone back into your life or make you cool enough to

attract a particular type of people as friends. If you expect too much, it has a crushing effect when you don't get what you hope for. Deal with the areas of your life that need to be fixed and understand that the major goal of minimalism is to help you live a less cluttered life and better manage your finances.

Chapter 4: How to Create a Minimalist Budget

So you're committed to becoming more minimalist, and you want to put your convictions to work throughout your life. You're ready to manage your resources around the minimalist philosophy. You're ready to create a minimalist budget.

Below is a carefully constructed outline to guide you through the process of creating a minimalist budget.

1. Have a plan.

The first and primary step of making any plan is to have a plan. Pun as it may seem, nothing can fall in place if you don't already have a mental picture of how everything should pan out. In the sense of creating a minimalist budget, the key thing is to have a plan for your finances.

The concept of the minimalist budget revolves around comprehending what you ascribe most value to and making plans to meet those goals. Like every other budget scheme, the aim is to meet target goals. But what sets the minimalist budget aside from all the others? In minimalistic budgeting, financing your plans comes from living a minimalist life. You practice living on less as a means of freeing up your finances to meet target goals. And unlike in other budgets where deprivation is sometimes employed to achieve financial goals, minimalistic budgeting entails nothing of the sort—you wouldn't end up sacrificing your satisfaction to meet your goals.

That said, let's return to planning. Before embarking on the journey to making a budget, you should consider some questions and analyze your answers. Such analysis should help you in your decision-making and planning.

Some questions to ponder include:

- What do you imagine your finances to look like in the long run? This question aims to give you a clearer picture of your goals.

- What plans do you have for the budget? Every budget is made to satisfy a problem, so what problem do you want to tackle? Do you want to pay off your debts or mortgage, save for retirement or a wedding, buy a house, or grow a business?

- Are your plans short- or long-term? Understand the nature of your plans. It helps to know how to go about your budget and what to expect in the long run. It's advisable that you write down your goals so you can easily access them and stay on track.

2. Outline your fixed expenditures.

After having a plan, the next important part of creating a budget is taking note of how much you use up within a specific period. It's best you outline your expenses every month. It makes planning more manageable, especially if you are a salary earner.

At the top of the list of your expenditures should be the fixed expenditures you make on repetitively, most commonly on a monthly basis. They do not include your voluntary disbursements and have to be made compulsorily. They include mortgage payments, transportation, childcare, rent, healthcare, and utility payments. These fixed expenditures should maintain compulsory slots on your minimalist budget owing to their relative importance to your wellbeing. Think of them as some of the necessities of life which must be properly budgeted for if you are to live and operate comfortably.

3. Take note of how you use money.

As much as we have evolved to use the words, "I don't know where all the money went" as a small fraction of our diction, it is essential we find out where we throw "all the money" if we are to succeed with a minimalist budget. The idea is to be mindful of our discretionary expenditures in order to channel our money into more important and useful stuff. That said, having outlined your fixed expenditures, it's imperative you identify your spending behavior. Not only will your knowledge of your spending pattern help you know how to spend wisely, but it will also help you control your finances, and budget more efficiently.

In all, it is essential you keep in mind that the expenses discussed in this section do not include your fixed expenditures. The expenses here refer to your discretionary spending, which tends to differ from time to time. To begin, outline all the things you spend your money on over a specific time frame—both products and services. It could be over a week, a fortnight, a month, etc. These expenditures could range from the frequency with which you eat out or how much takeout you ordered to how much you spent on dates in the past month or the number of times you have hung out with friends or how much you spent on clothes. If the expenditure is not part of your fixed expenses and you indulged it of your discretion, it is worth noting.

Tracking these purchases can be labor-intensive, but if you spend with a debit or credit card, you can check out your expenses from the financial statements on your credit card(s) or bank account. This is a helpful and effective way to track your expenses over time. To ensure ease of computation, you can set up a spreadsheet for entering your discretionary expenses. Moving on, sum up your total expenditure across your chosen timeframe and get the total. Make sure not to add your fixed expenses to your discretionary expenditure just yet. Having arrived at a total for these expenses now, you can enter your fixed expenditures into another column of the spreadsheet and find the total of both categories of expenditure. The total of both groups is the amount you have spent or are spending within a particular period.

You can go on to compare this total against your net income in a month. Check if it matches your income precisely, or is less or more than you earn in a month. Whatever the case may be, you have to properly evaluate your expenses to ensure they tally with your financial plans.

When evaluating your expenses, below are some tips you can ponder:

- Consider the necessity of the expenditure: Before making any expenditure, think about the thing you are about to purchase. Is it necessary to buy, or are you spending out of impulse?

- Consider the value of the expenditure: Ponder on the return on investment (ROI) of the expenditure. Would it better your life, or is it going to constitute clutter and a waste of vital resources?

- Consider the importance of the expenditure: Minimalism is all about focusing on the important, so if the expenditure holds no importance, it is both bad for your finances and your budget. Fixed expenses have importance and are necessary for comfort. On the other hand, unnecessary expenses could include discretionary spending such as impulsive shopping, binge eating, and the like.

There is no fixed amount of money to be used on discretionary expenses unless it exceeds your budget and strains your finances. As such, it is up to you to determine the amount of money that goes into voluntary disbursements. Just ensure that they would be beneficial to you in the long run and don't just promise short-term benefits alone.

4. Review and regulate your expenditures.

In the previous step, the total of your discretionary expenses and fixed costs might be equal to, more or less of your net income. If it is equal to or more than your income, there is a problem. If the total is equal to your income, you may not have the allowance to save for tackling contingencies. And if the total exceeds your income, you stand a chance of running far into debt. To avoid these nasty scenarios, you should begin by scrutinizing your discretionary expenses and setting out limits to curb overspending and destroying your finances.

Next, pick out any irrational or impulsive expenses and downsize your expenditures until only the necessary expenses are left. That said, the next step is to create a plan for regulating your expenses to fit into your financial plans. From here on, you can begin drafting your budget to align with the way and manner you want to allot your expenses. To improve your chances of saving a fraction of your income and maintaining your budget, it is imperative you spend way less than you make over a specific time frame. Some important questions to ponder include the following:

- Is there any similarity between your income and expenditure?

- Does your expenditure reflect how much you earn or does it reek of overspending and debt? Also, consider how much of your income goes into savings every month.

- Is your savings a significant fraction? If there is none, do well to make an allowance for savings in your budget. And if it won't amount to much in the long run, play it cool. The aim is to create a minimalist budget, so it's okay.

Go on to categorize your budget, and add limits to every category to regulate your spending. Below are some tips to help you out:

1. Review and regulate excesses.

After categorizing your budget, individually scrutinize every category based on your results from your previous expenditure. This will help you properly regulate your overall budget without going overboard on the minimalism train. For instance, review the food category in your budget. Did you get so much groceries in your previous purchases that some were never eaten and got spoilt? This is an indicator that you may have a little too much money budgeted out for food because you eat less than you acquire. That said, look out for skewed expenses within the categories of your budget and regulate them.

2. Review and regulate your wants and needs.

Sometimes, one of the biggest problems of humans is not knowing distinguishing what they want and what they need. Your needs and wants are two distinct phenomena in themselves. For instance, eating a chocolate bar with your lunch can be rather sweet, but is it something you want or is it a need? Is it fundamentally important to your existence, or is it just meant to satisfy a craving or impulse?

The ability to define your wants and needs is a quality character which could help you regulate your budget and set limits. In the end, don't forget to sum up all the numbers of all the extra expenses you have made.

3. Take stock of what you have.

When making your budget, it's advisable you take stock of all that you own. It will help you plan better by keeping you updated on the things you have as well as what you don't have. It will help you avoid arbitrary and overboard spending. You would be surprised how much strain you can relieve on your finances. Also, taking stock can help you downsize your possessions, keeping and pursuing only important things.

4. Go for long-term items.

The best way to enjoy the benefits of a minimalist budget is to go for products or services with long-term value. This way, they won't become useless or break down in the long run, and you will get optimal value for your money. For example, rather than spending your money on a vintage dress for a retro-themed outing, choose to buy a suit for work instead. The former has a short-term value of getting you into the party; however, the latter promises a long-term value by improving your wardrobe.

Long-term purchases are also inclusive but not limited to items used for multiple purposes. Multipurpose items are budget-friendly due to the financial efficiency they provide by serving multiple purposes altogether. They also tend to be eco-friendly because they produce less impact on the environment than different single-purpose items would. For instance, a water purification system would be of less impact on your budget and the environment than cases of water bottles. Also, dish towels are preferable to paper towels in that the former can be used and reused while the latter can't. Another example is items that can be refilled. Instead of buying new packs every time you run out, opt for refills.

Although there is no guarantee that long-term items will be the less expensive choice at first, when compared to their short-term options, they will provide good value in the long run and save you on extra expenses. Additionally, one goal of a minimalist lifestyle is reducing consumption and environmental impact. So even if you don't personally realize the benefit, your efforts can produce a benefit for the earth and society as a whole.

5. Review your plans regularly.

The concept behind a budget is to act as a guide for keeping you on track. To measure your progress and remain on track, you have to check the guide regularly. If you don't, you couldn't know when you are going off track.

As such, it is imperative that you schedule the time to go through your progress and review your plans every other week. Review your budget, classify your expenditures, and check to ensure you haven't gone astray with your expenditures. But why is the whole reviewing thingy so important?

Well, besides helping you remain on track with your financial goals, reviewing is essential for maintaining and regulating your budget, as well as owning up to your expenses, correcting any mistakes, and starting off the next period of your budget more intelligently. That said, it is advisable you take the time out to go over your budget regularly for the duration it lasts to be able to make subsequent changes as is necessary.

6. Simplify your finances.

Your finances should neither be as complex as rocket science nor as twisty as calculus. It should be something you can easily review and understand. The perspective that complex is sophisticated is just wrong. Simplicity is the best form of sophistication.

Find ways to downsize and simplify all your financial accounts. Begin by combining all your accounts into one to make management and accessibility as smooth and easy as can be. For example, two accounts—one savings and one checking, should suffice for your finances. If you have a different accounts with various banks, you can try to consolidate all of them to simplify the running of your finances. Also, if you have more than one credit card, go over their uses and importance to your finances. It may turn out you need fewer to run your account(s). Put away the cards that aren't of much use at the moment until you truly need them. In all, minimalism is key to creating a budget, and it will help make your finances easier to run and handle.

7. Plan your purchases.

"Failing to plan is planning to fail." Nothing states it better. Proper and regular planning is vital to your budget if it is to be efficient because contingencies are bound to arise and expenses will appear. But how can all these fit into your budget without driving you into debt? This is why you have to plan.

Your financial targets and your expenditures have to be in alignment to ensure the smooth running of your budget. If done otherwise, your budget could tank, and you could be in debt. To ensure none of these happen, you have to make adequate plans to make your future expenses mindfully and not on impulse. Before you fork out cash for any purchase, meditate on the usefulness of the item, its value quotient to your life and its effect on your finances. Is the item worth the bother? Would it be useful in the long-term? Was it budgeted for? Does it provide more than momentary satisfaction? It's imperative you question your motives for obtaining any item to ensure you only use valuable money on the needful and remain within the confines of your budget. You can also keep your financial targets handy by storing them on your phone or on a piece of paper stored in your wallet. This way, you can go over them before making any financial decision.

Chapter 5: Myths of Minimalist Budgeting

Like every other scheme in the world today, minimalist budgeting is not without its myths. Let's consider some below, and find out how reliably they hold.

Minimalist budgeting means deprivation

This stereotype is usually what scares people away from indulging in minimalist budgeting, but just how true is it? While it might seem valid because minimalism in itself entails downsizing, it is quite far off from the truth. If deprivation means cutting off everything which brings no value whatsoever to you and helps you achieve more with less, I dare say it's the right kind of deprivation. The minimalist budget aims to promote frugality and help you make more with less while staying focused toward your financial goals, not to aid deprivation.

Minimalist budgeting boosts your finances

First of all, it's imperative you understand that minimalist budgeting is a technique of budgeting and not a magic show of some sort. It isn't a scheme to take your finances to a new high. No. This myth is born of misconstrued knowledge of the uses and benefits of minimalist budgeting. One of the purposes of minimalist budgeting is to simplify your finances and help make ample use of your earnings to achieve your financial goals and live a simple, well-resourced life. For some people, there may be a noticeable "boost" in their finances; others will not. But that is all relative to your individual situation.

Minimalist budgeting is for people with financial problems

Choosing to simplify your finances doesn't necessarily imply that you have financial problems. Compare that thought to daily sanitation in a home. The home doesn't have to be a trash yard to be cleaned up by its inhabitants. The same goes for minimalist budgeting. It isn't exactly a ticket out of hell given to persons who need a way out from the problems plaguing their finances. Anyone can choose to indulge in minimalist budgeting at any point in their lives, regardless of whether or not they have immense financial power.

Minimalist budgeting is stressful and time-consuming

The rationale behind this stereotype is flawed. How is taking the time out to plan how best to put your finances to good use a stressful and time-consuming process? Just because it sounds too good to be true doesn't mean it's a string of complex processes that results in a headache. The idea is to keep your finances simplified, and the budgeting process in itself is very simple to carry out. You needn't have a diploma in accounting or be a calculus whiz to use minimalist budgeting. No. It's as smooth a process as they come.

Chapter 6: Some Basic Financial Principles

This final chapter is aimed at helping you better manage and grow your income. Forget what you may have heard—minimalism is not the same as poverty. The essence of minimalism is not having limited funds, but using what you have judiciously and with intent. Now that you have learned about minimalism and you know how to create a minimalist budget and stick with it, here's more on how to, if you please, correctly water your finances so that they grow. Try them out.

1. **Understand that money is a powerful force**: Having lots of money at your disposal may reveal a dark side to your personality you never even knew existed. If you used to be a frugal spender, you may become less conscious about how much money leaves your bank account. It is this decreased discipline that some translate as "more money, more problems." It is quite easy to develop a warped perspective of one's financial status when we start earning more. This calls for carefulness.

   From watching people flaunt their wealth and seem to be happy, there is a tendency to believe that having more money will make us happy like them. In truth, having more or less cash will not make you any happier than you were. If anything, it exposes the areas of your life that are lacking. Let money be a tool for you to enjoy more of life's experiences, increase your value, and make even more money. Try not to be carried away by your increased income.

2. **Let your money work for you**: It's good that you have chosen to spend less and save up a substantial percentage of your income. But if you decide to go by savings alone, it'll take more years than you have to spare before you achieve financial freedom. So, you ask, what then do I do with the money? Well, you *should* save some percentage of your income to prepare for unforeseen circumstances. But, you should also carve out another percentage for investment purposes. These may be either passive or active investments.

Today, technology has made things so easy that you can sit in the comfort of your home and put money in real estate, forex, gold, oil, and so on. You may even buy shares in some companies. You could decide to invest in your own business. Rebranding, advertising, and expansion cost a lot of money, after all. Putting money into the growth of your business is a viable investment option. Only make sure your money does not sit still and idle. Minimalism may be about getting only the things you need, but what if those things are more expensive than you can afford? Remember, it is not advisable to always go cheap, as this may cost you much more in the long run.

3. **Never stop educating yourself**: Whether it's about new frontiers in your line of business or in minimalism, you stop growing when you no longer pay any mind to self-education. Contrary to what education is commonly used to mean, in this context it has little to do with which school you attended or your acquired degrees. There is so much that you can learn from a single YouTube video about how to succeed in any aspect of your life than from years of formal education.

   Attend seminars and lectures. Connect with those who have succeeded on a path you are about to tread. Ask that they mentor you. The wheels of change move ceaselessly and quickly. Self-education will ensure you are always updated on whatever is current and more efficient. This increases your value and, as a consequence, your earning power. Also, if you are into the generation of passive income, you want to stay on top of every new investment opportunity. Educating yourself is also a part of self-development, and this helps you to enjoy life even more. It makes you a more fun individual to be around and opens your mind to greater possibilities. The benefits of self-education are so wide that one cannot possibly say no to it.

4. **Know how to treat your money**: If you manage your finances with the understanding of the importance of money, there is a greater probability that you will be able to multiply it. Truly, money isn't everything in life, and we have touched on that in this book. But money is essential to the quality of life you will have and can give to those who depend on you. Healthcare, a decent house, a good school, feeding, clothing, and many others are all passengers in the vehicle of money. Don't sabotage yourself with a mentality that money is evil.

Money is neither good nor bad. It is not sentient or alive, and cannot make choices on your behalf. It is true that one can get intoxicated with the power and luxury that money can afford. But, in the end, the choice rests with us. You have taken a step in the right direction by choosing this book to help you live with modesty and simplicity. This is not an excuse for you to stop putting your best into your job and to keep adding value. You should not hate money any more than you should love it—and you should not love it. Simply use it with intent.

5. **Giving is not losing**: If you are sure your personal finances can take it, leave room for donations in your budget. Embracing a life of giving is capable of bringing true joy to your life. Why do you suppose some of the richest and more famous personalities in the world give a large some of their wealth to different charities? Not all of them are for PR reasons. Sometimes, it is because your giving comes back to you sooner or later. We are all connected in this world, and the more people you are responsible for lifting out of poverty and suffering, the better for you, your family, and future generations.

   But do not feel you must do this when your finances cannot manage such expenses. Time is another commodity at your disposal, which you can give. You can also teach people ways by which they can fend for themselves. There is also volunteering and you can donate items you no longer use. Just make sure you give to your family, friends, acquaintances, supposed enemies, and as many as you can reach. Giving teaches us to be content and plants lasting seeds of happiness in our hearts.

6. **Always have a plan for the rainy day**: We never want to think that something bad could happen to us suddenly. But things never stay the same. Companies go bankrupt, assets depreciate in value, countries have

even worse economies, and people get seriously ill. It is unwise and unsafe to live without some strategy in place when things suddenly go south. These unforeseen mishaps may happen even if you try your hardest to be careful in all your dealings. Your best bet is to have some cash saved up in preparation for such times.

By so doing, you will not have to go into debt and affect some other area of your life because you weren't ready. You may even decide to have a different bank account for this purpose. This is all up to you. Do yourself and those dependent on you a favor and stop believing that life is one smooth journey with no detours.

Chapter 7: Debt

According to a study conducted by Northwestern Mutual, the personal debt owed by the average American amounted to about $38,000 (2018). And this figure appears to be on the climb. An article in USA Today reported that the average household debt in America is $137,063 (2017). People now possess as much as five credit cards, most of which are already maxed out. Before you go thinking this problem is isolated to America alone, the average household debt in the UK is £59,540 (The Money Charity, 2019). Going by these statistics, it would appear that there are more borrowers and debtors in the world today than savers and investors. To turn this around, the appealing exterior of debt must be unraveled to expose its ugly core. What good will the minimalist budget be to you if you still believe in certain myths about debt?

Debunking Common Debt Myths

1. **You shouldn't be afraid to stand as guarantor for your close friends and family members**: After all, it's your uncle. He's good for it. Turning down anyone's requests to co-sign with them for a loan does

not make you a bad person. There will no reasoning with the lenders if that uncle or whoever you are guaranteeing does not pay back. So many have fallen victim in similar cases. They are chased down and made to pay off someone else's debt. If you've got the money, give it to the person in need of a loan. But if you don't, respectfully decline and be firm in your choice.

2. **There is no way to get rich without, first, going into debt**: If you truly believe this, then it could be that you haven't done much digging for yourself. There are numerous stories of people who became millionaires without having to fall into the quicksand of debt. Gary Vaynerchuck, owner of VaynerMedia and motivational speaker, is one case in point. He worked his way to the top, and would always point to the following as the major keys to his success: not purchasing stuff he sees as dumb, living on the barest minimum, and saving. If you do a little research, you will find numerous stories of wealthy individuals who made it, but never fall into debt.

3. **It's alright to loan money to friends and family**: No, it's not. In fact, when that close friend or family member next comes to you for a loan that would really affect your finances negatively if not returned on time, be resolved in saying no. Of course, you love

them. You want them to be happy, and they may have been there for you in the past. But money has a way of changing the dynamics of any relationship, regardless of its strength. If the debtor is unable to pay back for whatever reason, it would cause them to feel shame. You, the lender, becomes the master and they, the slave. Here's what you should do instead: give. As opposed to lending money, giving is not a business transaction and typically nothing is expected in return. If the person wants more than you can reasonably part with, then give what you can and explain that it is the most you can do at the moment. Just don't let people you care for be indebted to you in this way.

4. **The average person needs a credit card**: They also say teenagers can learn to be responsible and disciplined individuals if given credit cards. These are all lies that were created to keep you trapped in the system. Credit card companies are not built with the interest of their customers at heart. Instead, they sell you an illusion and, unknown to you, tighten their chain around your neck. By the time you wake up to what is going on, you've sunk so deep that you lack the courage to even imagine your way out. If anything, credit cards encourage young adults to be materialistic and to go about life without a plan. These are not things you want your kids to mature into.

5. **No country's economy could survive a completely debt-free culture**: First, this is only a consideration because of how deeply entrenched debt is in our society. For many of us, debt is a concept we have witnessed since birth. Whether it's a mortgage, car payments, credit card payments, or student loans, we just cannot fathom a life outside some kind of debt. Secondly, the country may initially be destabilized, but it would be a sacrifice worth making in the long run. People would learn to live within their means and would swap debt for a culture of savings and investment instead. It would also result in lower crime rates and a happier society in general.

Why You Should Avoid Debt

1. **Think of your credit score**: Lenders will check your credit score to ascertain how much of a risk you are or if you pay back and on time. Depending on what they find out from your credit score, they may or may not give you the money you are asking for. If they do agree to lend you some money, it might be significantly lower than what you had asked or it might come with very high interest rates. This becomes a problem when you are

looking to become an entrepreneur. Despite the viability of the business, how knowledgeable you are in the field, and how few competitors there are, it would amount to little if you don't have the capital and no financial institution is willing to loan you the money because of you poor credit score. Sadly, simply paying off your debt may not do much to improve your credit score. It is always better to avoid debt altogether.

2. **Credit cards encourage you to live above your means**: Since this book is now in your hands, it is the assumption that you have given minimalism some thought and would like to gain more knowledge on the subject. You may then decide to give it a try. But, doing so and using credit cards may be counterproductive. You will find yourself constantly torn between the ideology of minimalism and the promise of your credit cards, one suggesting you live with simplicity and the other saying there are no consequences to living well above your income. Don't tempt yourself by thinking you can get away with doing both. Your credit card will most likely win out in the end. The reason for this is that minimalism is at first painful, but enjoyable in the end. Having a credit card is all pleasure in the beginning, but may be painful later on.

3. **Those bloodthirsty interests**: When it comes to debt, every financial institution functions in much the same way. Yes, there are some differences but, typically, the more money you owe, the larger interest it gobbles up. So, with each credit card swipe and each loan you receive, your income becomes increasingly smaller for you and your family. It costs money to be loaned money. And that cost, more often than not, only ever goes up. Should a debtor continue sinking further in debt, soon they'll be using 100% of their income to pay back, and this may not even be enough.

4. **You may never be financially free**: Elusive as financial freedom may be to many people, it is even more so to those in debt. This is because debt thickens over time and covers whatever ray of hope you may try to get out of the debtor's life. If you are one such person, you may have resigned yourself to the endless loop of minimum payments, ever-increasing interest rates, and unpaid bills. Your goals of owning a home, going on vacations, and living without financial worries may now seem like a pipedream. Here's something else. Even if you start earning more, you might be trapped psychologically and never make a move to get yourself out of debt. Instead, you just keep buying more.

5. **Negatively affects relationships**: More valuable to our wellbeing than money or materialism are the relationships we foster. The unconditional love from our spouses and kids and the ready support of friends counts for much more than expensive objects or the approval of people who care nothing for us when we purchase such items. Why would you want to sacrifice joy in place of passing fancies? Being in debt strains relationships to the point of permanently breaking them. You may find yourself constantly arguing with your spouse, being absent from your kids' lives, and never wanting to do things with your friends anymore. Such a life is lonely and empty. It is always best to try figuring out a different solution for your problems instead of falling into (further) debt.

Debt Denial Symptoms

Are you in debt denial? It's possible to be completely submerged in debt and still believe it is not as threatening as it looks. The best way to never get out of a problem is to deny the fact that you have one at all. But sometimes we may be completely unaware of the fact that we are in denial. That said, below are a few ways to identify debt denial.

1. **Things will be fine:** It's just a little debt, you say. Many people have had it worse and still bounced back. Sooner or later, things will right themselves. These are not, necessarily, the wrong thoughts to have. But the problem is thinking everything is going to be alright and not having a strategy to get yourself out of that bind. You've got to have a plan. When the going gets rough, we sometimes fall into a habit of lying to ourselves about the seriousness of the situation. But, for the sake of your mental and emotional wellbeing, acknowledge the fact that you are in debt and recognize how bad it is. Then, go ahead and solve it. We'll talk later about several ways to get out of debt. Hey, writing a minimalist budget is one way out of debt. Think about it.

2. **You get into quarrels and even lose friends over money**: Do a little retrospection today. Ask yourself the reason why you stopped hanging out with that person who used to be so close to you. How about your currently strained relationship with your spouse? Can you determine the origin of the problem? If it has anything to do with debt, then you may have been in denial all this while. It could be that you asked a friend for a loan, but were denied one. Has your spouse been trying to encourage you to save more, and you feel guilty because you have been lying to them about your crippling

debt situation? Not every relationship outlives debt.

3. **You take unmitigated and uneducated risks**: You don't even care to determine the level of risk you are taking. You invest in different schemes without performing due diligence or throw most of your money into gambles. If you find yourself in such a situation, could it be that these are desperate attempts to get out of debt? Right now, you are so taken by the idea of a lucky break that you do not even question anything. If you spend so much time in debt, what seems like the way out may in fact be a way to dig yourself deeper.

4. **You give in to various vices to get your mind away from your debt**: Drinking, smoking, substance abuse, and the likes are often merely symptoms of a larger and more crucial issue. Debt is one such issue that may cause an individual to go into a downward spiral. It may be that you have concluded that your debt problem is an insurmountable one, and the only way, it seems, for you to keep moving on is to find a way to shut out thoughts related to your debt crisis. Still, the problem does not actually go away and this, as stated in the second point, results in strained relationships.

5. **You say it's good debt**: First and most importantly, no debt is good. But there is a difference between life-sucking, predatory debt and debt that promotes an opportunity. It's *always best* to avoid going into debt for such opportunities and investments, but such debt is merely bad and not life-sucking. If it's a student loan, then it (usually) goes toward training that should boost your earning potential. Additionally, the interest rates for student loans are not very high, and in the US you can receive small benefits in your income taxes while carrying student loans. Mortgages are another example of debt that secures something of lasting value. Your credit card debts, on the other hand, are the life-sucking ones. The interest rates are through the roof, and all you get is the opportunity to fill your life with objects you don't really need and ensure you stay a debtor for a long time. Car payments and personal loans are also bad debt.

6. **You open new credit cards when the old ones have been maxed out**: You keep digging yourself in to get yourself out. If you have more than three credit cards, then all signs point to you being in debt denial. Why else would you open a new card, unless the old ones now get declined at point of sale? You go out with all your cards in your wallet, and try one after another in hopes that one just might work. You avoid the thought that

you now owe five or even six-figure debts and rationalize your actions by believing you will pay it all within a few months. Usually, the situation is more serious than that.

7. **You don't have a budget:** Are you the kind of person who receives their monthly income and just wings it? If yes, it may also be safe to assume that more than 40% of your income is used to settle debt. Basically, you live from one debt to the next. Without a budget, you have no map with which to navigate your spending. Very often, it is those people who are in debt who don't see a need to write a budget. But there *is* a need to write one. After spending what you will on debt, what remains still needs to be handled with intent and wisdom. Having a minimalist budget ensures that you take care of your debt, pay your bills, and, if there is anything left, get what you need.

8. **You only pay the minimum**: And this is why you don't bother to think about how much you are owing. You pay the minimum every month and convince yourself that you are using the money of whichever financial institution gave you your credit card. Here's the thing: only paying the minimum ensures that you never attain financial freedom. In fact, banking institutions and credit card companies love customers like that. They've got a name for them, too: revolvers. This is

because, with every minimum payment, the customer's balance keeps accruing interest. And, as such, a minimum paying customer may never get to break the cycle of debt they find themselves in.

9. **You are saving none of your income**: Ever noticed that people who are in debt are more likely to get into more debt? If you had cash in hand, you would use it rather than swiping the credit card. Yet because they believe that everything is going to be alright, they pay only the minimum, spend freely, and move on with their lives as usual. Either there is not enough left to save or there is no sense of urgency about having a savings safety net in the event of unexpected circumstances.

10. **You purchase items you have no need for**: Write a list of ten things you purchased recently with your credit card. Now, how many of them were above $100? Also, how many did you truly need? Better still, after writing out these ten things, check the balance on your credit card(s) to know how much you owe. People who live above their means will in no time run into serious debt. And to keep their lifestyle, they may lie to those around them about how much debt they owe. Even worse, they could tell the same lie to themselves and never get around to dealing with the problem.

11. **You are scared to look at your credit card statements**: Are unopened bills strewn about your office table? How about your mail? Do you have a long list of unopened mail about bills and various debts that are yet to be paid? If you answered yes to these questions, then you are not only in denial but also living dangerously. Simply looking the other way will not make the problem go away. But you have made a wise choice in purchasing this book. You don't have to keep thinking there is no solution to your debt crisis. If you've got a job, then start drawing up a minimalist budget for your finances. Be resolved to live as a minimalist and use the financial principles given in the next chapter to help you get back on your feet again.

Chapter 8: Tips on Saving Money as a Minimalist

By now, we know that the lifestyle of a minimalist centers around saving money. And it creates a more effective relationship with our finances. Being a minimalist already means that you will not be spending as much as you would otherwise, but you can still stretch the little you spend even more and save even further. Sure, it sounds impossible, but it is possible with the right mindset. You will be able to save effectively even in your new lifestyle. Just like everything in life, when you practice enough, it then becomes part of you.

These are tips that are proven to be effective for saving, even as a minimalist, because like it or not, we all need to save one way or the other. Being a minimalist is not an excuse for not saving. In other news, the tips include:

1. Reduce space.

Try downsizing. The reason why you may be spending more than you need to each day is that you are living in a big house with an outsized portion of what you earn going into your house. That can easily be avoided by having a smaller home. If you don't have a lot of family members, there's no reason for having a big house; the extra rooms and sitting rooms are far from necessary.

This is one of the reasons why both minimalists and non-minimalists have a very hard time saving. In this case, your own house is the one eating you out of money and a home. Think about that.

2. Get a roommate.

Get someone with whom you could share the house expenses. This will help you save a lot because you can divide in half the money required from you to run the house. With a roommate, you get half of all the house expenses and also a companion you can engage in different activities to from time to time. Of course, it is important you find someone who shares the same or almost the same values as you. If you can do so, you will have little to no problems living with that person as you share common ground.

3. Avoid eating out all the time.

When you eat out all the time, you spend a lot of money without even knowing it. You will save a lot of money simply by getting some groceries and cooking your own meals. Many of us spend a lot of money going out to eat, and most times we forget the effect it could have on our finances in the long run. If you calculate how much you spend on takeout each week, it would probably be more than enough to prepare something in your home that would have lasted you longer. You will have to plan and prepare, both of which take time and effort. But if you have free time, then there is nothing stopping you. And as mentioned previously, the benefits of cooking for yourself are such that you may derive more value from doing it than from spending your time on other activities. You have to evaluate and make the smart choices for yourself.

4. Assess whether you need your car or not.

Think about your day-to-day routines and find out if you can still commit to those routines if you did not have a car. If you can, there is no need having or keeping the vehicle. Sell the car and use the money for something more productive because that car needs to be repaired from time to time which means that you are losing money. Then there is the cost of insurance, and sometimes you would need to take the car to a car wash. These are expenses that can easily be avoided simply by selling the car and using the money for something that you identify as a true need.

5. Buy more frozen foods, fruits, and vegetables.

You will save a lot of money buying frozen foods because they will never go bad when they are frozen But when it comes to fresh fruits like berries, after some time they will eventually go bad. Many people think that when you buy frozen fruits, you don't get all the required nutrients, but it's a lie. If you do your research very well, you will find out that fresh fruits are picked before they are ripe in order for them to be transported without them going bad. But frozen fruits are picked and frozen when they are already ripe. That's important because ripe fruits and vegetables are at the peak of their nutrient density. So if you want to talk about nutrients, you can get as much or more from frozen fruits and vegetables. So don't be deceived.

These tips should help you save more like a minimalist. All you have to do is to know where your strength lies and focus on it.

Chapter 9: How to Build Discipline

There are certain principles to success in life that are just indisputable and non-negotiable. One such principle is discipline. We're not born with this virtue and thus have to work on building until it becomes a part of our character. Sometimes it feels like we are not in charge of ourselves and have little control of our actions. Regardless of how much you want to stick with the minimalist lifestyle, so much will come up to distract you and deter your resolve. You must have observed this trend lots of times in your life and in the lives of others. The initial momentum of doing something different and new slowly wanes and you find yourself back to the old habits you had sworn off. This is because habits are neural pathways etched in our brains from certain repeated behavior.

The tips in this chapter are intended to help you take charge of your life and do what you know is right, even when you don't feel like it. The more you practice them, discipline will be ingrained into your very nature as new neural networks are formed in your brain.

1. **Find the time to meditate**: Today's world is so fast-paced, we can barely find the

moment to relax besides when we fall asleep at night. You can start to take back control of your own rest by meditating. When you do this, you should avoid any other thoughts, despite how important they might seem. Concentrate your mind on either your breath pattern or heartbeat. Because you have gotten so used to moving about and being engaged in some activity, it may prove difficult to sit still for the first time you try. But this is not a reason to give up.

When you meditate in the morning before going to work or beginning your day, you are relieved of stress and worry. You are less hurried, and can process information better. This makes you a lot more efficient at whatever you do. Don't be worried about having to spend so much time meditating. You can be done in about 15 minutes and still enjoy nearly the same benefits as one who meditated for an hour. When it seems like your mind is starting to wander to other things, make it focused again. Meditation is a crucial discipline that will help you develop the focus and attention needed to be disciplined in other areas of life.

2. **Be grateful**: Like meditation, make a habit of doing this every morning. Often we can't control our actions, such as impulsively buying things, because we are dissatisfied with what we have and think that packing our

lives with material things will make us happy. This attitude to life is the result of a failure to realize how good we have it compared to other people. While you worry about not being able to afford a designer shirt, there are millions of people who cannot afford to buy shirts of any price. Accept that a change of perspective is necessary, and start working towards this mental shift.

Instead of bothering with whether the glass is half-full or half-empty, you appreciate the fact that you've got a glass and there's water in it. This also functions as a reminder when you feel moved to act in old patterns and start acquiring stuff you don't need. When your focus leaves thoughts of lack and moves to gratitude for what you do have, you become less worried and, consequently, less stressed. As such, you can work on becoming more disciplined in other equally important areas of your life. Also, stress can be harmful to your health. Gratitude is a guaranteed drug to combat it.

3. **Watch the foods you consume**: Yes, you have to be disciplined about what goes into your mouth, but did you know that eating unhealthily can affect your ability to be disciplined? It takes energy to stay focused. The kind of food you eat will largely determine how well you will be able to stay focused or if you'll be easily distracted. If

your diet is comprised mostly of processed foods and you barely ever eat things like fruits and vegetables, the body will spend the greater amount of its energy digesting the meal and you will have little left to do anything productive.

Also, the amount of food we consume is important. Eat too little and you will feel tired after only a short time of exerting the smallest effort. If you eat too much, you will feel lazy and sluggish for the most part of the day. Eat the right type of food and in moderate quantities and you'll have the strength to stay focused and the presence of mind to practice discipline in every area of your life. Eat more organic foods and meals prepared at home. Create a plan for what you eat. If you do these things, you will notice a spike in your energy levels and have the potential to achieve your goals.

4. **Exercise**: How often do you work out? Like minimalism, exercising takes discipline to start and see it through. If you can be committed to a workout lifestyle, it will afford you important and necessary lessons to be disciplined in other areas of your life. Now, when you imagine exercising, the picture that first comes to mind is probably one of a muscular giant of a man pumping iron and sweating it out in a gym. This is a stereotypical way to view exercises. But even

something as simple as a brisk 10-minute walk every morning can do wonders for the heart and keep the body in shape. People go to the gym largely because of the encouragement of seeing others workout, too. But you can save membership fees and do sit-ups, push-ups, jog, or exercise with a jump rope right in your house.

The benefits of exercising are so numerous that one needn't look for any other incentive to start. When you work out, your heart rate goes up. This means that more blood circulates throughout your body and your body cells will have as much oxygen as they need. For this reason, you will be less prone to illness and, because of the increased production of dopamine and serotonin, you will also be less stressed out or worried. Your mind becomes more efficient at focusing on a task or the achievement of any goal when you exercise.

5. **Up your sleep time**: Plentiful sleep is more important than many people realize. A large percentage of us barely get five hours of sleep everyday and this can be detrimental in more ways than you know of. Matt Walker, in his TED talk, pointed out that sleep deprivation can lead to all sorts of harmful consequences. He listed anxiety, depression, infertility in men, and susceptibility to a wide range of

illnesses as some of the things brought about by lack of sleep (Walker, 2019).

On the other hand, sleeping well aids in memory retention. This is good because you want to always remember the motivation behind your choices, like deciding to be a minimalist and working on your discipline. Plentiful sleep also contributes to more energy and less pain because your body is able to repair and heal itself when you sleep.

This is why you have to rid yourself of so many vices that hinder your sleep. Smoking too many cigarettes in a day or consuming high amounts of alcohol can affect how quickly you fall asleep and the smoothness of that sleep. Also, it is not a good idea to have caffeine less than six hours before going to bed.

Even though we like to brag about the sleepless nights we have sacrificed for the sake of our success, the entire purpose may be defeated if one does not have quality health to enjoy the rewards.

6. **Don't let up—persist**: If you have read at any time or were told by anyone that the road to becoming a truly disciplined person is without its challenges and obstacles, you were terribly lied to. When you decide to relearn habits that have been a part of you for

years, you may often feel like giving up. It may seem like you are not making any progress and you may think that minimalism just isn't for you. But if you can readily identify what living without a culture of discipline has cost you, then you will be more motivated to hold firm to your resolve.

Many things that are truly good for us in the long run do not provide their rewards immediately. We usually have to go through much pain. It is this grueling process that solidifies the position we have taken. So don't give up. Everybody fails at something. It is persistence that distinguishes those who never make it in the end from those who eventually reach great heights.

Progress is often unnoticeable at first. While you're still thinking you've not moved from the same spot, you may not notice how effortlessly you do the things that used to demand a lot from you. Keep trying.

7. **Plainly define your goals**: Don't be vague about the things you hope to achieve by adopting a lifestyle of discipline. With respect to this book, your desire to be more disciplined should be with the aim of sticking to your minimalist budget. You want to be more thrifty with your money and also have a less cluttered home. Whatever your goal, make it simple and to the point. If it'll make

it easier for you to always remember, write it boldy on paper and have it on the wall in your house. Let it remind you of the fact that the way you used to do things was inefficient and that going back is not an option.

Many times, people don't set goals because they hop on the bandwagon of a new trend and try to come up with goals passively. This attitude of rationalizing our actions after the fact is mostly unsustainable. It is why we fall off the bandwagon as easily as we got on it. Before you start on your journey to becoming a minimalist and after you have understood what that entails, you should outline your goals. They should be measurable and simple. By doing so, you may find the needed strength to keep forging ahead at those points when you feel like calling it quits and accepting failure.

8. **Organize your life:** If you have any kind of personal relationship with truly disciplined individuals, then you must have noticed that they also seem to love order. There is a correlation between people who have mastered themselves and organization, and this may be due to the fact that one may not achieve the level of discipline they aspire to by living chaotically. For this reason, you are encouraged to declutter your home, office, and mind. Also, have a routine for actions that could be classified as tedious and

repetitive and a schedule for the more important ones.

Start small, as that might make it easier for you to get through organizing all you need. If everything in your life has its place and your activities for any day don't just crash into you, you will be able to achieve a more relaxed state of mind and body—all things that are good for building discipline. It cannot be overemphasized how important focus is to developing a character of discipline. If your life is one haphazard mess, where you are always looking for different items and cannot tell what you should be doing at any particular point in time, you will find yourself restlessly in motion. You will not be able to understand yourself, let alone master your life.

9. **Take out the temptations**: If you are trying to stop a particular behavior, it is wise to stay away from whatever acts as a trigger for such actions. Sometimes, these things are not triggers, but are what we run to for whatever reason. In other words, such things are what we hope to wean ourselves from. Some people, to avoid spending so much, might put their money in fixed deposit accounts. You might also want to unfollow certain social media accounts that showcase the beauty of luxury items and that enchant you with such pictures.

The less often you see such pictures, the easier it will be to develop your self-discipline. Otherwise, it would simply feel like an annoying case of continuously running around in circles. You cannot hope to change any habit when you continue to feed your mind with the old information that spawned that habit in the first place. Take away the distractions and remember to replace them with things that are in line with the growth of your self-discipline. Instead of following the glamorous and mostly unreal lives of celebrities on social media, choose motivational speakers who promote an attitude of prudence and minimalism instead. And there are a wide number of them to choose from. Stay focused on what is best for you.

10. **'Fess up about your weaknesses**: Ever heard about emotional intelligence? You will need to work on it to develop self-control and discipline. One of the questions you will have to ask yourself as you build up your emotional intelligence (or EQ) is this: how well do I know myself? More often than is necessary or safe, we lie to ourselves. We refuse to acknowledge our weaknesses. This may be because we are afraid of being taken advantage of. In like manner, we may also refuse to accept, point out, or celebrate our

strengths. A reason for this is that we might be seen as proud.

But self-awareness is one of the most important steps towards managing yourself successfully. If you do not accept the fact that you are weak in a particular area, then you may not do anything to avoid the related temptations or work towards becoming stronger. Your weakness might be an addiction. Do not claim that you can control it if you want to. Do some introspection, and if it turns out that certain habits have, indeed, been in control of your life, you can now work on disciplining yourself. Some weaknesses which drive some individuals to choose minimalism include being people-pleasers and having a shopping addiction. What are your weaknesses?

11. **Believe in yourself**: You can place a limit on how much you will achieve. It all begins in the mind. You know when people say that your life is merely a reflection of what goes on in your head? It turns out there is some fact to that belief. A study was done to test the limits of the average person's willpower. It was discovered that if a person believes they can hold out for a very long period, it is unlikely that they will give up soon. But those who already limit themselves in their heads find that they cannot hold out for too long (Job, 2010). This means that whatever

chances there are that you will weather a challenge are determined, first and foremost, in your mind.

Going by this knowledge, you are the greatest factor, positively or negatively, to achieving your goals. If you can get out of your head and believe in the limitless potential of your willpower, you will move on regardless of the external factors that try to stop you. You will not always have people to remind you that you can achieve all you set your heart to. Sometimes you have to believe in and motivate yourself. Spark your zeal when you start second-guessing.

12. **Have a backup plan in place**: There are certain situations that just might be outside your control. Say you absolutely must go with a friend to shop for clothes and you have a penchant for purchasing expensive, designer clothes, even though they will hurt your finances. Do not leave yourself totally exposed and then berate yourself afterwards for giving in to passions you hope to change. First, explain your new lifestyle choice to your friend. Next, go with them but leave your credit and debit cards at home. Always have a plan in place for as many eventualities as you can think of.

Going into any situation with a plan will help you stay focused and maintain a disciplined attitude. Sometimes, this plan may involve restraining yourself as in the example above. Other times, it could be that you have to find an alternative and shift the focus of your mind to this. This is not to say that a backup plan will make it easier to stay disciplined. There is still some work to be done in keeping to the plan. But it ensures your mind is not engaged in a battle of self-growth versus pleasure. Once the plan is set, you need only go along with it.

13. **Reward yourself each time you show discipline**: Prizes are not only given out to make the winner feel good about themselves. It is also done to motivate the recipient of the prize to put more effort into achieving the same or an even bigger level of success next time. If you are a parent reading this, then you probably understand this very well. Parents often reward their kids with more TV time and the like for doing something right. Pet owners also utilize this idea to promote good behavior.

Rewards also give us something tangible to look forward to. It increases your passion and causes you to work a lot harder than you would have. The reward doesn't have to be anything grand or expensive. Simply treating yourself to a nice outing may be enough. If you have been holding back from making impulsive purchases, you can pick one item with a price tag that is within your minimalist budget and buy it. This could be a new pair of shoes or a new tie. Reward yourself at different intervals and for different accomplishments to encourage the growth of your self-discipline.

Chapter 10: Tips on Becoming a Minimalist

These pointers will assist you with all that is necessary to begin your minimalist journey.

1. **Schedule some days for decluttering**: Get your calendar and figure out those free days. If you can't find any, then you might need to create some. Assuming you work a 9 to 5 job from Monday to Friday, you've still got Saturdays to declutter and Sundays to do nothing but kick your feet up. Also, decluttering needn't last an entire day. 10 to 15 minutes should suffice. Remember, your goal is not to, in one fell swoop, organize and tidy your entire house. Select and dedicate certain days to decluttering, and be committed to spending a minimum of 10 minutes on those days doing exactly that.

   If you need to download calendar applications to stick with your planned routine, then do so. Make sure that during those scheduled periods, you do nothing else besides decluttering the particular area of your home you have mapped out for the day. Also, make sure to let your family or those sharing the house with you know what you'll be doing and that you would prefer, at those times, to not be disturbed. It is not fair to assume they would know to leave you be during those times. Communicate your schedule with them and plan out family time, too. That's very important.

2. **Buy less, and choose high quality**: High quality here should not be translated to mean expensive. As a minimalist, you should look out for products that are long-lasting. Your objective is not to follow a trend or show off your designer wares. Still, this is not asking you to be cheap. Learn to strike a balance. Read the ratings for the product you are about to purchase before paying for it. If all there is to be said about the product is how ridiculously pricey and popular it is, then you should look for a different brand. There are products of good quality that can be had for decent bargains. Seek those out.

Also, do not make buying a frequent occurrence. You are trying to conserve money by being a minimalist, and such a purpose is defeated if you are constantly buying stuff. This is one reason why you should buy products of high quality. If they can survive a few months or years of use without fading in color, having tears, or decreasing in efficiency, then you will save the cost of replacing it. Even though you're not advised to spend exorbitant fees for any item, you just might have to if it's worth it, quality-wise. Instead of going cheap, look for discounts and cash in on those. Take an event like Black Friday as an opportunity to purchase discounted items.

3. **Be sure you need an item before making a purchase**: This is one of the most basic principles behind minimalism. If you do not have a clear need for it, you should reconsider purchasing the item. And do not shortchange yourself by trying hard to come up with a reason why you need that item. If it doesn't come to you almost immediately, then avoid buying it. It is unlikely that this item would go out of stock in every store in the world, so take some time. If it later occurs to you why you should purchase the product, buy it then.

   As a minimalist, you should learn to spend with intent. Don't click buy on every trendy and appealing product advertisement which comes up on your screen.

4. **Pack light for any travel**: Maybe you've never given it a try, but you can have as much fun traveling light as when you carry three heavy suitcases. Sometimes, all you need is a small-sized bag. Even better, a backpack might suffice for the entirety of your trip. There are quite a number of things in your bag that you will, in all likelihood, never use

during your vacation. Also, you need to know how to pack for different types of trips. If you will mostly be going to the beach, then you will need a swimsuit more than a parka. Along with not having to exert so much energy pulling heavy luggage to and from your trip, you will also save money by traveling light.

If you don't have a small suitcase, purchase one. The excess space in large luggage might cause you to keep adding more items, even after you have packed all you need. Also, do not rummage through your belongings on the day of your trip for the things you need to pack. Have a list ready days before the big day, and pack your suitcase the night before. In this way, you won't start throwing in unnecessary items simply because there is some space left, and you won't need to do your packing in a hurry.

5. **Learn how to cook**: This is beneficial to your health, the quality of your life experiences and your finances. Learning how to prepare your own meals also gives you the satisfaction of knowing all that went into the food. You can guarantee that it is clean and healthy in every way. You know those elegant dishes in magazines and on TV? There are free recipes available online for a variety of meals. There is every possibility that you will find the recipe for your favorite dish on one

such site. Don't be afraid to try out some of them. Your first try might not cause colors to burst as you close your eyes in satisfaction, but you will get better at it. Just keep practicing and trying new things.

Cooking is a way to relieve tension. After the hustle and bustle of trying to make a living, there are few things which rival the relaxation of cooking your food. It is also good for your mind, as you are growing your knowledge bank and increasing your skill set. Also, you don't have to search in futility for the kind of food you are interested in at a particular moment. All you need to do is buy the ingredients you need and make it happen in the kitchen.

6. **Be content and appreciative for all you have**: We mentioned this earlier when discussing discipline, but it is crucial and should be reemphasized. The wants of any human being are without limit. The more one has, the more he realizes how much more he wants. Our needs, on the other hand, can be met. And this is why the principles of minimalism urge you to place your needs in focus and pursue them instead of your wants. Contentment has little to do with dressing in an orange robe, sitting in the lotus position in a monastery and meditating. Although monks are good teachers of minimalism and contentment, you can choose to be satisfied

with the things you have without moving into a monastery. The problem might be that you see all your possessions like an app—you're always looking for an upgrade.

If you believe in a god(s), then thank whatever deity you serve for the people in your life and the things you are able to afford, as you wake up in the morning. If you do not subscribe to any religion, understand that not many people in the world enjoy the things you claim are not enough for you. Just the fact that you can make up your mind to choose minimalism is enough to be grateful for. There are a vast majority of people who have nothing or less than what would be sufficient to live on. These individuals are not blessed with the luxury of choosing to live with less. Be content.

7. **Look for hobbies to replace your shopping time**: Sometimes, the reason why we buy so much is because we do not have a lot going in our lives to keep us occupied. Yes, you've got a job, you love going to the cinema for a good movie and some popcorn, and you hang out with your friends from time to time. But there are those times in between when we get bored, lonely, or sad and start thinking that buying something new will make us happy. You get excited at first, but this feeling doesn't last very long. So you buy another, and the cycle goes on.

Find yourself a hobby that isn't so expensive and that completely engages your mind. It could be yoga, guitar playing, mountain climbing, and so on. When you spend so much of your time doing something that makes your truly happy, you'll have less time to lose money acquiring new stuff. If you're into poetry, attend slams and perfect your poetry writing or performance skills. Also, this will take your mind away from buying things that are essentially useless and you will channel your purchases toward your passions instead. You just might find that you are more interested in having an art studio or buying a chisel for your next sculpture than purchasing an iPhone X.

8. **Have a clear vision for choosing minimalism**: Unless you chose minimalism because you thought it was a fad and you like to jump on trends, then you must have had a reasonable objective to opt for a minimalist lifestyle. If you had none and just thought minimalism would make you look cool, you should define your goals for changing your lifestyle in this way or you might lose the will to continue.

This tip holds true in every aspect of life. Habits are difficult to turn. When all you have ever known is how to spend most of all you earn and fill your life with materialistic things of all kinds, you may find it increasingly difficult to maintain a lifestyle where you're supposed to think that less is more. Figure out what you hope to gain from minimalism and let that hold you up when you're about to give up.

9. **Learn to respectfully decline gifts and other free products**: The "buy one and get 3 free" ads should have less allure for you. Unless they concern products like detergents, where having extra might come in handy for future use, simply take what you need and be on your way. You don't need free stuff if you already have a sufficient enough amount of that item at home.

    But businesses are not the only ones who will try to give you free stuff. Some family members or friends may think of you and buy a wristwatch, clothes, kitchen appliances, and so on as a gift. It can get a little tricky trying to turn down gifts without hurting others' feelings, but there are ways to go about this. You could, graciously, accept the gift but also let them know that as a result of being a minimalist, you really don't need more than two wristwatches. Thank them for the thought and ask if you can give it to someone else instead. Another way is to thankfully accept the gift and let them know that, in future, they might have to ask before buying you a gift. Lastly, you could politely say no and explain why to them. This works more times than you would imagine.

10. **Don't subscribe to every magazine and newsletter that catches your fancy**: After reading that captivating online article and seeing the option of subscribing to the blog's newsletter, do not be in a hurry to do so. Minimalism does not only concern your physical situation. Digital clutter can be a far greater stresser since we spend so much time relying upon the digital world, and there is little getting away from it. Things like emails can be clutter and become a source of distraction. As such, be picky about the websites you subscribe to. In this way, you will be able to keep up with the messages that enter your inbox.

This advice follows for physical mail and magazines. If you find your mailbox getting filled, deal with it quickly. In line with controlling your magazine and newsletter subscriptions and organizing your mail, you should also make sure to keep your house free of used papers. Also, old documents that will no longer be of any relevance to anyone should be shredded and discarded. Such activities would also be helpful in decluttering your mind (yes, your mind gets cluttered too).

11. **One item should go for another to come in**: This is a good way to keep living with just the bare minimum, without having to continue with old, inefficient, and worn-out items. You should keep a specific number of any particular item and try your hardest to never exceed those amounts. If, for example, you keep just five shoes, then you know that one pair of shoes will have to be given out or discarded to allow you to get a new one.

    Indeed, this system may not work in some instances. And you do not have to follow this method when you are starting. But the more time you spend as a minimalist, the easier it will be to handle your possessions in this manner and the better you will understand which items should be managed like this and which should not.

12. **Consider borrowing, instead of buying**: There is a chance that many of the things you buy for short-term use are owned by your neighbors or those you share a close relationship with. Why spend money on something you will most likely use just once and store away for months or years? How about you rethink buying every single tool you'll need to fix the pipes underneath your sink or those you might need for gardening. The same thing goes for books. These are the reasons why you should purchase a book: it is not available in the libraries close to you, you

will use it for a very long period, and it's so good that you will keep opening it from time to time. If it doesn't fit into any of these reasons, it would be better to borrow the book from the library.

13. **Online shopping is better than the traditional kind**: This may come off as a contradiction to some of the points earlier stated, but it couldn't be more true. As distracting as shopping online might be, there is a decreased chance that you will lose track of what you had come to buy and start perusing other items. This is quite commonplace when shoppers go physical shopping. You are face-to-face with several different items all at once and the products are not just pictures with price tags. The allure to purchase stuff you don't need is much greater in a physical store than in an online one. You can simply type in the specific products you want in the search bar, add them to your cart, and make the payment.

14. **Some sentimental items have decorative purposes**: You don't have to purchase a rare minimalist painting at an auction in order to decorate your house. Remember your kids' first drawings? Frame those. They will do just fine. You don't have to beautify your home for the fleeting satisfaction of impressing visitors. This is not

to say that if you truly admire some piece of art or decorative item and would love to have it in your home, you must restrain yourself from doing so. If it is within your minimalist budget, then you should go right ahead. But, it might be much better to have decorations to appeal to your emotions, encourage you to continue on your minimalist path, and remind you of family and friends.

Chapter 11: Decluttering

We tend to pay no mind to how the state of our houses affects our productivity or mental and emotional health, but worry instead about how they appear to others. For this purpose—keeping up appearances and people-pleasing, that is—we try to have *everything*. Paintings, more chairs than we need, more food than is necessary in the refrigerator, and so on. Usually, the first step of minimalism is getting rid of such things—especially, when you have no need for them. But this is not exactly decluttering. Clutter is used to refer to those items in any home that are not organized or take up space that would fit a more useful and functional item or purpose.

There are various ways to go about the decluttering of your home. The two most popular kind at the moment are KonMari and Swedish Death Cleaning. Below are some of the advantages that decluttering can have in your life.

Benefits of Decluttering

1. **Saves time**: If you have decluttered your home, you will find that you spend less time looking for things. A cluttered space makes

for numerous hiding places for the little things in your house. It doesn't only happen in the movies. In real life, keys do have a way of pulling a Houdini when you are in a hurry. Then there are other things like toothpastes, pens, earrings, and, of course, needles. Decluttering your home means that you have organized every item in your house in such a way that everything has its place.

2. **It gives you a sense of accomplishment and self-confidence**: Decluttering can prove to be a very challenging ordeal. Since you are not supposed to attempt to complete it in one day, it will require some level of discipline for you to stay committed to the task. Every day you don't give up should be registered as a win in your mind. You will also be faced with the task of making some crucial decisions: to discard or not to discard. This is a good exercise for people who may not esteem themselves highly and are always doubting their capabilities. If you can pull through with decluttering your house, it will afford you enough motivation to take on any other challenge.

3. **You never know what forgotten treasures you might stumble upon**: This is often the case when decluttering your home. Items from weeks, months, or years ago that are still useful (probably more so

than ever) and that you had forgotten were still in your possession may suddenly be rediscovered. This is not to say that you should always expect such occurrences whenever you decide to declutter. But if it does happen, the pleasure that rides on the backs of such discoveries are often worth whatever energy you had exerted. Imagine finding some cash in your pockets or a note you had written in a sudden burst of inspiration?

4. **Mend relationships**: If clutter happens to be something that causes you and your spouse to be at each other's throats, then find the time to declutter and see what happens. A messy home has the tendency to create rifts in even the most loving families. Spouses blame each other for not taking the initiative and being responsible enough to keep things in an ordered fashion, and this anger may be transferred to the kids too. Sometimes, there are other underlying factors to blame for the disagreements, but you may never know what they are until you take the step to declutter.

5. **It can get you out of debt**: This may seem a little unreal at the moment, but consider it. How did you get into debt in the first place? Was it by purchasing the things you didn't need with money you didn't have enough of? If so, then decluttering can put an end to this

pattern of behavior. After you have discarded the things you do not need and that are no longer useful, your home will look so calm and spacious that you will feel compelled to sustain this new look. This means that whenever you want to buy something new, you will wonder about its position in your house and question if you truly need it. Another way decluttering can get you out of debt is by garage and eBay sales. Items that can still be put to use but which you do not need can be sold. The profit from such a venture can be used to clear your debt.

6. **You will find it much easier to clean your house in future**: That first total decluttering of you house will save you from a lot of future stress. Next time you want to tidy up your house, there will be less stuff for you to go through. You will be done in no time with cleaning your house compared to when your house was cluttered with unnecessary things.

7. **There are tax benefits to decluttering**: Not all items have to go to the thrash when you clean out your clutter. Some things may still be useful and, as such, should be given as donations. And what do you know, these donations are considered tax deductible. In other words, you would pay less in taxes and

have more of your income to invest, save, or do whatever you want.

8. **Decluttering gives your mind something else to do**: If you notice that you've been worrying a lot, you might need some healthy activity to get your mind off that thing of concern. Organizing your home can be very engaging, not just physically but also for your mind. Unlike other destructive actions like smoking, binge eating, or drinking, you get to be productive in the process of decluttering and might even come up with a solution to what bothered you.

9. **Sustainable happiness**: This comes as a result of no longer relying on things for your happiness. You will attain a higher level of satisfaction when you can be rid of that item that you have effectively placed above yourself. You will then be able to realize that lasting joy is a result of the relationships you water and the memories you make with those you care about. You will also be less envious of other people and can truly appreciate and enjoy what you have.

10. **A less cluttered mind**: There are other factors that must be put in place in order to enjoy a clutter-free mind, such as journaling and prioritizing. But decluttering your house is definitely one good way to start. An organized and spacious house will allow you

breathe and relax. Now that one thing has been checked off the to-do list in your head, you will be able to focus better on other tasks. You will also find less things to distract you.

11. **You can go green with less clutter**: If you are conscious about polluting the environment, then you must wonder a lot about the effects of your sizeable garbage and its effect on the environment. Less clutter and less stuff in your house means less garbage also. It also means that you can choose to consume less of those things that are harmful to the environment. You can take back control of your house and no longer be at the mercy of objects.

Chapter 12: Is Minimalism Boring?

This is a question asked by a lot of people. The question comes with a lot of views and opinions.

Many people think that being a minimalist means that a person is boring or lives a boring life because of certain things they do, say or even the way they act. Some people fear to go into the minimalist lifestyle because they feel that as soon as they start that lifestyle, they automatically become boring. But you should know that it's not true. The reason why people have these ideologies is because of various myths and false stories passed around about minimalists.

A lot of us must have heard some of these stories before, while some of us haven't. Here are some of those oft-repeated stories:

1. They believe that they do the same thing every day: A lot of non-minimalists believe that minimalists have the same boring routine every single day. They believe that minimalists have a calendar that they follow and a routine that they can never depart from. They have this idea that falling away from your routine does not make you a minimalist anymore. The bottom line is that they nurture the mindset that minimalists are neither fun nor versatile.

2. They believe that minimalists wear the same clothes every day of their lives: They think that minimalists have the same wardrobe, year in and year out. They believe that they can't be versatile enough to wear a different kind of clothing, sticking to one style of dress all year. Some people might look at minimalists and think that they don't change their clothes or even buy new ones. Why? Because they feel that minimalists want as little clothing as possible in their homes to reduce the risk of clutter.

3. They believe that minimalists don't buy fancy or expensive things: This is a belief that a lot of people have about minimalists. They believe that they have the money and or finances to buy whatever they want but hold back because they are greedy. They think that minimalists have the money to live the high life but decide to stay in the low. This is another reason why people believe that they are boring. They think that they cannot use their own money to have fun or to treat themselves.

4. They believe that minimalists eat the same type of food: Be they vegetables, proteins, fruits—you name it. Some people believe that minimalists have no taste for other types or kinds of foods except the ones that they eat and are used to. This is one of those myths that still makes its rounds amongst non-minimalists who are considering the minimalist lifestyle. They think that minimalists are boring people who will never be versatile enough to eat another kind of food. Eating the same kind of food is not a bad thing, but non-minimalists have attached it to being boring or living a boring life.

5. They believe that minimalists do not change their cars: Now, this is a funny one. Some people believe that a minimalist will drive the same car for as long as it lasts. And the thought of having a highly dated and eventually worn-out vehicle is unfathomable. This myth is a great example of how non-minimalists jump to rash conclusions about the impracticality of minimalism. The reality is that some minimalists will find ways to live a life that doesn't even require bothering with a car while others will determine that having a high-quality, worry-free vehicle makes life infinitely easier.

6. They believe that minimalists are judgmental jerks: For some people, there is an implied rebuke or protest in the way minimalists live their lives differently from the mainstream. Especially if someone following the minimalist lifestyle has the resources to spend lavishly, they may seem stingy, and their reluctance to acquire material things may be viewed as a protest against conspicuous consumption. Many people get uneasy when others don't do the same things they do and instead adhere to their own principles.

7. They believe that minimalists are mindful about how much they spend: Each of these myths has been boiling down to the fact that minimalists do not like spending their money, no matter the situation. They think that minimalists will spend money only on things that are essential and needed. They also believe that a minimalist will not spend their money in ways that are thought of as fun. They think that because of their "boring" lifestyle, they can never enjoy their money to the point that it benefits them and others.

These misconceptions are the tools that make non-minimalists judge minimalists. Being a minimalist does not mean that you are boring or that you don't spend money. It only means that you watch how you spend your money, you watch how you buy things because the more things you buy, the more clutter you have. The reason why a lot of people have clutter in their homes and or offices is that they buy things that they don't need or never needed. Those things then end up creating a whole lot of clutter in your home for no reason, which means that you took your money and bought yourself a whole lot of mess. This is what they try to avoid. By monitoring what you buy and in what qualities you buy them, you will be able to keep your space in order at all times. Because fewer things mean less clutter, and less clutter means less stress, and less stress means a healthier and improved way of life. This is what non-minimalists fail to understand. If you are hung up on any of these myths, you should look beneath the surface to see the importance of certain things.

The reason why people make up these cock and bull stories is simply that they don't want people to be minimalists at all. This is something that many see and believe, but it's not their fault; they believe whatever they hear regardless of who told them or the facts that accompanied the news. These myths are still making their rounds in conversations discouraging the minimalist lifestyle. This should not discourage you from being a minimalist; being a minimalist could help you understand things that you have always taken for granted.

So if you have decided to develop a minimalist lifestyle, block out any influences of non-minimalists. You might think that you are confiding in your friend or family member about the change in your new lifestyle, but there is a high possibility and or probability that they are not going to be in support of it. There is also a chance that they might do all they can to discourage you. They might even tell you most of the myths and false stories listed above. You now must know what you want and stand by it.

Being a minimalist is all about creating space for the important, and it's also about giving a hundred percent focus to anything that you involve yourself in.

With all this said and done, why still ponder on the question "Is minimalism boring?" To put this question to rest once and for all, let's consider why people think that minimalism is something boring in the first place.

The main reason why people think that minimalists are boring is because of their way of life. They live a simple and low-profile life, which means that they are not always noticeable. Society accepts and adores a set of people who can do the extraordinary, who can make things happen with their status. They love people who drive sports cars, live in nice houses and wear the latest fashion. That's why everyone wants to be a movie star, and just a few people want to be minimalists. This is a very wrong ideology. You should know by now that you should never judge a book by its cover because when you do that, you throw away every possibility of knowing that book for what it truly is. Same goes for minimalists; they are people who see life differently from others. They dwell more on the important and focus on what needs to stay by letting the unimportant go. This may seem hard, but you should know that nothing perfect comes easy.

When people tell you that minimalists are extremely boring, they are saying that because they are seeing minimalists from the outside all the time. Or not at all; they're merely responding to their own impression of what a minimalist is without ever having met one. They judge minimalists from the outside. You must look at the benefits of minimalism before listening to the nay-sayers. Minimalism is a way of life that many people do not understand. Try and get someone to completely explain the concept to you (preferably a minimalist) and then you will be better equipped to reflect on the minimalist lifestyle. You might even think that the world would be a better place if it were full of minimalists. But who knows?

The question "Is minimalism boring?" has not been answered fully yet. Most people base their conclusions on the wrong reasons. These people have a wrong ideology about what minimalism is. They think minimalism is boring because they consider people who do it to be people who do the same thing over and over again. They think that their whole lives are centered on just one aspect or thing. This is far from true. Minimalism is one of the most productive and interesting lifestyles we have on this planet.

Minimalism helps you get in a state of mind that you would have never imagined yourself in. It opens your mind to a lot of possibilities. It shows you the good, the bad and especially the ugly. It exposes the consumer-driven life you have been living and tells you that you have been living it the wrong way when you thought you were living it the right way. It shows you a whole new life that was in front of you all along, but you were too stubborn to embrace. This could help you even in your place of work by opening your mind to new ideas. How? Being a minimalist means you are free of clutter, which means that you are free of stress, meaning that your mind now has more room to access all the ideas that come into it. Minimalism is a way of life that is taken for granted by a lot of individuals in the world.

You have before you a great opportunity, an opportunity that will take you to new heights. Yet you doubt it because of silly rumors and speculations. Now that you have the power in your hands, you can use it the right way because just like they say "with great power comes great responsibility."

We've been beating around the bush about whether minimalism is boring or not, but minimalism is far from boring. How can something that enables such progress in the things that matter be boring? Minimalism makes things easier and makes high levels of personal productivity easier and faster. The last thing you would want to do is to underestimate the power that comes with minimalism.

In conclusion, if you want to be the very best at what you do, you need to put your priorities in order. How? That's simple. It's by doing these:

1. Having a few good and trustworthy friends: friends who will share your vision and encourage you throughout, not friends who will eventually pull you down with their personal agendas.

2. Have few things in your possession: own a few things that you need and not just things that you feel must be in your space.

Like it or not, this is a way of life that is one of the best. If you are reading this and till now you are skeptical about being a minimalist, it's because you are really scared of how much you will enjoy it when you finally get into it. Don't think about what people would say. Only think about what your lifestyle would say for you.

Chapter 13: Handling Relationships with Non-Minimalists

Becoming a minimalist is a choice and should not be forced on anyone, no matter what. When people decide to become minimalist, they can be discouraged by friends, family members, or even their spouses. When someone as important as your partner does not share the same value for minimalism with you, it poses a challenge in the relationship. Some relationships could either be affected in the wrong way or destroyed. This doesn't mean that living with a non-minimalist is impossible; it only means that specific steps and precautions should be taken to effectively live with someone who doesn't share the same values as you.

The steps below will help minimalists and non-minimalists live together in a healthy, productive, and nonjudgmental relationship. Consider putting the following tips into action:

1. Don't allow things as little as individual belongings come between both of you.

The fact is that when you are a minimalist and your partner isn't, you are bound to get frustrated at some point. When he or she is not doing what you want and how you want it, you are will naturally feel overwhelmed. But you should know that this is the first step that destroys certain minimalist and non-minimalist relationships. You should learn to make the other person understand the reason, the why, that you need things done in a certain way. And if they love you, they'll seek to understand and adjust because they recognize that it's important to you. You chose to go into minimalism because of a reason, and you tend to be committed to that reason. You also chose your partner for a reason, and you should not let something as small as material things come in-between the both of you. You should be committed to your relationship as much as or more than you are to minimalism.

2. Try to stay away from his or her items or belongings.

When practicing minimalism, you will have the urge to declutter your space. Be it your kitchen, bedroom, or even your living room. But you should know that you share those spaces with someone else and some people don't like their things moved around without their permission, and that is what causes a lot of disputes in relationships when it comes to minimalism. You should start with your own stuff, especially when your partner is not around. Once your partner notices and acknowledges the difference as it applies to your stuff, then you can begin to declutter when your partner is around. Let your spouse be aware of anything that you do in the house. The good communication will show respect and consideration, and it will strengthen your bonds. In time, you may be able to join forces to apply your minimalist lifestyle to all of your home and the whole of your life together.

3. Allow your new lifestyle to show its importance.

Your spouse, parents, or friends may not be in support of your new lifestyle, but you should try to make them understand by your achievements. How? Your new lifestyle will bring a lot of advantages; all you have to do is to let those advantages speak for themselves. Your space will look more inviting and remarkably free of clutter. When they see that, it will help them understand your reasons for going minimalist. It might even make them want to join you. So the bottom line is making your success speak for you. This could make your partner understand you and your decisions better.

4. Try to come to a rational conclusion about certain things.

Sitting down and talking is going to help you come to a rational conclusion about certain things in the house. Both of you should try and come to an understanding about decluttering or even rearranging. There is a possibility that both of you could understand the new lifestyle better and adapt to it more effectively by doing these things. Sitting down and talking could help you resolve a whole lot of problems. This is one of the most straightforward tips and the most effective.

5. You must be patient.

This is extremely important. Before you try any tip at all, you must be extremely patient with your spouse. Forcing them to do anything is just going to backfire. This is a life that you want for yourself, but you are sharing your life with someone else, someone who will not like having that lifestyle forced on them. Being patient with them helps them understand that you want the best for them. This strategy can work magic. Just be calm, not overbearing, and let them take in the minimalist lifestyle at their own pace. The bottom line is don't force it.

6. Try to explain yourself.

The key to all of this is to get your spouse to understand you, and you can do that by thoroughly explaining yourself in a way that your spouse will understand. Most times people fail to completely explain the benefits of minimalism to their spouses because they think either that it is obvious or that it doesn't hold much relevance, but you should know that it is more important than you would have ever imagined. At this point, all you have to do is to sit your spouse down and explain everything bit by bit, no matter how long it may take. Consider the doubts that they may have, and find ways to specifically address them.

7. Never force change on them.

Change is constant in the life of any human being, but that change cannot be complete if that change is forced. That change can also not be enjoyed if it is forced on them. Being a minimalist is contagious, after spending time with a person who is a minimalist, you are bound to pick up one or two things from them. You have to sit it out and watch them slowly get involved in your lifestyle by themselves.

8. Try to ask them for help.

If you have successfully succeeded in convincing them, you could ask them to help you to do different things to help you add to your success in the minimalist lifestyle. All you have to do is to ask them to help you politely, and if they genuinely love you, they will willingly help you get to what you want. You should know that someone who truly loves you will never try to pull you down. Instead, they will do all they can to build you up.

This could also work when they refuse to be minimalist because you can never force the lifestyle on anyone. Even without them being minimalists, they can help you get what you truly want, which is being a true minimalist. This is probably one of the best and most effective ways of getting your family, friends, or even spouse to effectively accept this way of life.

They could help you clean, declutter, and rearrange some certain areas in the home and or office.

9. Set some boundaries.

If you did not succeed in getting others to either adapt to the lifestyle or help you in adapting to the lifestyle, you could easily set some boundaries in the house.

If they are kids, you could tell them to take their clutter to their rooms, a place where you can't see it. If you can enforce a rule like that in the home, it will reduce the children's clutter in many areas of the home. When they notice that the clutter in their rooms is getting too much, they will willingly give minimalism a trial. All you have to do is sit back and do nothing but watch them naturally embrace the benefits of minimalism.

But if they are adults, you likely share some spaces in the house, especially if both of you are housemates. All you have to do is to let them know about the particular portions of the house that are yours and that you need those places to be completely clutter-free and you will see that they will slowly understand why you chose the lifestyle.

The main aim of this tip is to reduce the areas in which other people in your home can create clutter. If you limit space for them in the home, they will have no choice but to declutter because sooner or later, their clutter would want to take over every space they have left. Limit their spaces and watch the magic happen on its own.

10. Try and embrace the outcome no matter what.

We are not superhuman. We are never capable of convincing everyone we meet. If you are unable to convince your loved ones with all your efforts, you don't need to get worked up and angry because they don't see reason and agree with you, all you have to do is accept them for who they are. Just let your examples speak for you and remember that they might not be in support at first. Many people never actively support something the first time they have a glance at it. All you have to do is to give them time, and if they are truly meant for that lifestyle, they will eventually come around. Getting yourself worked up because you did not get through to them is only going to throw your efforts out the window.

These tips and tools should be able to effectively help you live with a person who is not a minimalist. If you follow the steps in the right way, you should be able to adequately handle non-minimalists without getting angry, sad, or even frustrated. But you should always remember that forcing someone to become something he or she isn't will not help, even if those people are children. It's only going to make matters worse for you later on in life. Just wait and watch. They will join the lifestyle when they want to. But if they don't, you have to live with it because as you must know by now, no one is perfect.

Chapter 14: 30 Days to Minimalism—A Simple Guide

Day One

1. To begin your walk in minimalism, you have to start with the primary step of changing perspectives—a paradigm shift. You need to become enlightened to the world around you to understand properly your impact and place in it.

2. You have to understand that living with less gives you a chance to live more. When your perspectives change, so will your life. When your mindset shifts, you will begin to realize that less is more.

3. Organize your space. For the first day, begin with your kitchen. Starting here is important because it is much harder to maintain the kitchen or keep it decluttered than any other area of the house.

4. Keep in mind the number of utensils, cookware, and appliances used in your kitchen. Cut down on excesses.

Day Two

1. In the words of The Minimalists, "Consumerism is not a through street if happiness is your destination" (Nicodemus & Millburn, 2015). Before extensively going minimalist on your stuff, take the time out to search yourself. Know and understand what you stand to gain from minimalism in the long run. What is your definition of happiness? This knowledge could be what keeps you going.

2. Go through your wallet(s), purse(s) and bag(s). If there are too many of them, keep the ones you use the most and do away with the others.

3. Cultivate the habit of cleaning these items out every other week. Why is the bubblegum wrap from Monday still in your purse? Why do you still have that expired ATM card in your wallet?

Day Three

1. Figure the value quotient of your stuff. Your possessions should either bring you joy or serve a useful, long-term purpose. This should be your go-to thought before doing away with your stuff or bringing in newer items. Consider how useful the item would be or has been to you. Did it serve a

long-term purpose, or was it to satisfy an immediate need?

2. Turn your attention to your closet. Classify your clothes. That is, make different categories for tops (shirts/blouses), bottoms (trousers/skirts/shorts), and undergarments.

3. Go through each classification and categorize every item into two piles—keep and discard. Put the clothes you use into the keep pile and those you seldom ever wear into the discard pile to be donated or discarded.

Day Four

1. Begin your day on a positive note. When you get out of bed, make your bed immediately. You would be surprised how such a small task can have a positive effect on your day. Your day gets better when it is begun with positive steps.

2. Go through your undergarments (boxers, pants, socks, bras, briefs, thongs, etc.) and do away with the ones that are torn, slackened, or worn out. Learn to get rid of things that have worn out or hold no value any longer.

3. Having done that, check your remaining undergarments. Take note to get newer ones if they are greatly thinned out.

Day Five

1. Develop a morning routine. In addition to making your bed every morning, identify up to five tasks you would like to incorporate into your morning routine. The tasks could be reading, writing, organizing, cooking, exercising, yoga, meditating, etc. You probably will not be able to achieve all five within an hour or before you have to get ready for your day, but doing at least two of those tasks should have a positive impact on your day.

2. It's time to hit your shoe collection. Go through your shoes and take out the ones that are outgrown, worn out, uncomfortable, or disliked. There is no point keeping shoes you no longer wear lying around. Donate or discard the ones that fall into any of the aforementioned categories.

Day Six

1. Take out the distraction. What's a distraction? Anything that gets in the way of important things is a distraction. Sleeping is an important part of your life as a human, so you shouldn't jinx it because of distractions. Keep your TV out of your bedroom, and don't attempt to use your phone when you hit the hay. The bedroom is solely for sleeping or

getting intimate. Catching up with work or your favorite show is just going to ruin the day for you tomorrow. If you break that principle, you will wake up late or tired and may not be able to practice your morning routine. Avoid distractions when it's time to sleep!

2. Go through your beauty kit. Go through your makeup case, creams, scents, hair products, etc., and do away with empty containers or the ones you no longer use.

Day Seven

1. Make decluttering fun. Understandably, people sometimes have sentimental attachments to their stuff. In this case, letting go may be quite difficult for them because of the finality of the process. However, letting go can be made easier, turned into fun even, when these people are assured that their stuff will go to help others. You can erect a donation closet for your household to make letting go of stuff easier.

2. Pay a visit to your dresser or drawers and clean out your accessories. Fish out any accessory that is no longer useful or is damaged and do away with it. Broken glasses, incomplete earrings, damaged belts, defunct wristwatches—fish them out.

Day Eight

1. Slow down. Stop. Breathe. This is arguably the best advice you'll get. The world is full of people who are so busy; it's a miracle they remember to breathe. We are gradually slipping into a rat race in which our lives are governed by outputs and rates and figures. But even as busy as we are, we don't earn enough for it. Why is this? Well, it's largely because there is a difference between being busy and being focused. Being focused entails being mindful and intentional about the important. Being busy, on the other hand, entails the basic trappings of busyness.

2. Go through your stash of prints; newspapers, magazines, comics, etc. Do away with them as they age. Almost everything can be found online now, so there's no point holding onto clutter.

Day Nine

1. Instead of throwing the stuff you no longer need into the trash, consider other uses for it. Try reusing and recycling these things, or you can donate or gift them to people who need them. You will contribute to the betterment of another person's life and improve yours at the same time.

2. Go through your shelves or stacks of books. REview your notebooks, textbooks, and novels. Discard notebooks that are of no use. Donate or sell textbooks and novels you no longer need. Doing this can help reduce pests and rodents.

Day Ten

1. Although this may sound extreme, the most proficient way to keep your stuff organized and downsized is to do away with most of it. Rather than perform organized hoarding on both the stuff you need and don't need, it's best you cut down on excesses so that you can focus on more important things.

2. The next stop to visit in your organizing spree is your CD and DVD racks. Take down all the CDs and DVDs you no longer use. If it's been ages since you slotted in that CD or DVD into a player, it's best you take it out. It's just contributing clutter.

Day Eleven

1. Don't fall prey to consumerism. Consumerism comes in different shades. Although minimalism advises keeping things spare and purchasing things

only for their importance and financial value, the point isn't to cash in on every sales promo. The sales price is just another facade of consumerism. You'd be surprised to find the item sells for way cheaper elsewhere.

2. Organize your documents. Take the time out to leaf through your stash of documents. Store important ones properly and discard the used ones.

Day Twelve

1. Declutter your vehicle. It's one thing to have a disorganized home and another to have your vehicle looking like a bomb site. You can incorporate it into your daily morning ritual to clean out your vehicle before getting into it. Clear out the trash lying around, organize your compartments, and store your documents properly.

2. Go through your stationeries. Keep only the useful ones and discard the dried out and dysfunctional ones. There is no point leaving around things that don't work if all they do is constitute clutter.

Day Thirteen

1. Don't get caught up in stereotypes. It's sad that the world swarms with stereotypes of varying sorts. However, you must ensure not to be caught up in the stereotypes of minimalism. Anybody can decide to live a simple life without being a Buddhist monk or Gandhi. Don't let others discourage you from achieving your simplicity goals. At the same time, resist the urge to cast judgment upon people who don't live the way you do. Do your thing, and celebrate it, but avoid the negativity.

2. Take a trip to your bedroom and bathroom next. Go through your sheets, blankets, towels, washcloths, etc. Remove the ones you don't use anymore as well as those that are worn out or torn. Do away with them.

Day Fourteen

1. "My house is looking scanty. Now what?" If you are at this point and have feelings of disappointment, this is for you. There's nothing wrong with having empty space. Truthfully, it is both fulfilling and beneficial to your wellbeing. How's that? First, don't confuse clutter with fulfillment or satisfaction. You don't need things to

bring you happiness. Your happiness is within you. On the other hand, clear spaces make it difficult for rodents and pests to harbor and breed.

2. Go through your cleaning products. Do away with empty containers. Opt for refills instead of getting newer products. Also, when restocking, go for eco-friendly products.

Day Fifteen

1. Resist the urge to hoard everything. You don't need to get something to enjoy it. Consider the material things of life to be like the cinema. It's a lovely experience being in one, but you don't see anybody going out of their way to get a cinema so they can have that experience anytime they crave it. Learn to experience the moment and make memories. You don't need material things to remind you of an experience. Memories over memorabilia.

2. Go through every piece of furniture lying in your home. Go through your dresser and shelves and wardrobes. You'd be surprised how much garbage is tucked away in them. Get rid of bad or broken furniture you can't fix or don't need. Also, downsize on the number of furniture items in your home; it's a living space, not a town hall.

Day Sixteen

1. Embrace a life of tidiness. Living with less means your space, finances, lifestyle, etc. is going to be both tidy and organized. You may have some adjusting to do, especially if you had tons of stuff and had trouble staying neat or organized. There are times when you might seem so free and unhooked it could get unnerving. But not to worry. Welcome to the upside of life.

2. The next destination to hit should be your pantry and refrigerator. Clear out any old, spoiling foods as well as those you don't want to eat. Gift foods you wouldn't eat to others who would, and trash the bad ones.

Day Seventeen

1. Practicing minimalism shouldn't be limited to your finances and home alone. You can also practice minimalism in your workplace. Clear out your desk and keep your desktop decluttered. One sure way to be productive and achieve more at your job is to keep your desk free of clutter. By so doing, there will be little to no items to serve as distractions, and the stress caused by clutter will be reduced if not eradicated.

2. To further enhance your productivity at work, try going through your devices and clearing out apps and files that you don't use. Not only will it make your devices faster, but it will also save on battery life.

Day Eighteen

1. Did you know that some of the healthiest people lead simple lives? Take a look at some of the wealthiest persons in the world, for instance. Forget the fact they live in a million-dollar homes; some of them have simple possessions and lead very simple lives. They do have the money to make all their dreams come true, but you don't see them reaching for everything and anything that catches their fancy.

2. Declutter your mail. This goes for everyone who has an email address. Go through your mail in your spare time and clean out the trash. Delete old and spam emails and leave the important ones. This will save you from distractions at work and useless pop-up notifications. Keep your life within and outside the internet organized.

Day Nineteen

1. Get some skills. You would be in a better position to practice minimalism if you learned some life skills that could help you with living on less. For instance, you may find it challenging to stay on budget or reduce hoarding stuff if you trash your kitchen and decide to live on takeout. That's not minimalism. Learn some skills like cooking, basic stitches, cleaning, and organizing. You'd be surprised how much you would save doing these tasks yourself.

2. Go through your subscriptions and unsubscribe from any service you are no longer interested in. Be it on cable TV, mail (emails and letters), social media, etc. Take a pass on the availability of clutter.

Day Twenty

1. Organization is a vital part of minimalism and staying tidy, especially after downsizing, when things begin to look scanty. This is why you have to be savvy when it comes to organizing. Make ample use of your storage, and do not be afraid to get imaginative when organizing. For instance, you can upcycle an old trunk to serve as a chair too. This way, you have combined two functions into one

item.

2. Clear your head. Sure, you are decluttering your space and leading a simple life, but what about your mind? Is it still strung out with stress and tiredness? Take the time out to relax your mind and body. Do the thing you have wanted to do for a long time. Go swimming. Knit that sweater. Get a perm. Just do that one thing that makes you happy and relaxed.

Day Twenty-One

1. Analyze your habits. Perhaps you haven't noticed yet, but your life is made up of many different habits (good, bad and ugly) which are done with or without your consciousness. And although we sometimes perceive them as factors that don't affect our lives, they do and in many different ways. Changing your habits means making a conscious attempt to take control of your life. Review your habits, note the ones which are neither beneficial to you nor others and try to change them one step at a time.

2. Take advantage of coupons and discounts. Instead of buying your foodstuffs in units, buy in bulk instead. As long as you're not overspending, this is the way to get the lowest price for most anything. This way you spend less and don't go overboard on your budget.

Day Twenty-Two

1. Evaluate your mobility options. Your preferred mode of transportation depends on several factors such as the distance you are traveling and your financial power, but what if you can save on transportation without inconveniencing yourself? Having a car can be expensive, as can taking rides using private transport companies or public taxi systems. Analyze your options of mobility and identify the one that serves you the most. The idea is to get to your destination; if the most inexpensive option can get you there, take it. There's no shame in going around by bus. If it were, no one would go by bus, and the bus system would be out of business.

2. Shop smart and thrifty. Visit wholesales stores for cheaper deals, and redeem your coupons on the valuable and important stuff.

Day Twenty-Three

1. Analyze and understand your motives for acquiring things. Your motives are divided into two categories, namely needs and wants. A good many times, our desires are the driving forces behind our actions. And unless we step up to the point where

we can analyze our desires and understand our needs from our wants, we may yet continue to wallow in habits we don't like. Minimalism involves knowing your needs and going for them instead of your wants because they are the more important option. Knowledge of the nature of your desire helps maintain a minimalist lifestyle, avoiding clutter, and engaging only in the meaningful.

2. Shop right. Every category of products has a market peculiar to it. There are food markets, meat markets, appliance markets, etc. If you need something, it's advisable you get them at their respective markets because they are offered at lower prices there than in multipurpose supermarkets.

Day Twenty-Four

1. Learn to be self-sufficient. The ability to fix your problems is no doubt a superpower, that much you should believe. Do you know how much you would save if you didn't have to pay for everything? Think about it for a moment. Imagine you grew your vegetables, fixed your car, and powered your home with renewable energy. You would be saving a ton of money. Apply this knowledge to every area of your life. So, instead of running to the tailor to get a button fixed, grab a sewing kit and get down to business instead. Learn to service your vehicle

yourself. You can apply this principle to many things.

2. Review the things you spend your money on and pick out the ones you can do yourself. Rather than waste valuable money on mediocre coffee at a coffee shop, brew your coffee. Make your own homemade cleaning agents and save on fanciful and expensive cleaning products.

Day Twenty-Five

1. Nearly every one of us has had the dream to grow up, hit it big, and become famous. Our parents envisioned us that way and implanted the image in us until we began to see it too. And while that was never a bad thing, a good many of us still struggle to achieve those dreams. We sometimes forget dreams aren't fixed points. They evolve as we grow. And while this isn't an anecdote to make you give up on your dreams, it's a reminder that it is okay to let go of some things. Press on your brakes and analyze your life. Is it better than it was when you first had the dream? Chances are you are living the dream without knowing and chasing shadows. Take the time out to absorb and appreciate how far you have come.

2. Clean out and organize your countertops because they give a messy impression. Organize items that

need storage into jars, and dispose of those that are worthless. Don't leave everything out on the countertop.

Day Twenty-Six

1. Since minimalism focuses on the important aspects of life and getting rid of the irrelevant, anyone who practices it is sure to get a good deal of time to themselves. This is possible because their attention turns from things with little to no value to the things that feed their values, freeing up their time to spend on their relationships, hobbies, etc.

2. As much as decorations are a thing which help set the mood for the holidays, they also contribute a large percentage of clutter. As such, your space is better off without them.

Day Twenty-Seven

1. Take little steps towards teaching others to live and stay organized. Sometimes, being a minimalist can be tough if you fly solo. Thus, to increase your chances of succeeding at the practice, try to incorporate the people living with you into the practice. Get them to organize their stuff for a

couple of minutes before bed.

2. Extend your tidiness to your digital life as well. Go through the files and whatnots that fill your gadgets. Delete the irrelevant ones before arranging the ones you use. Create folders to organize them into groups of related files.

Day Twenty-Eight

1. Sometimes, the problem is that you're so focused on acquiring material wealth that you make poor decisions on how to use your time. You should set tasks which are important as priorities for your everyday life. It's preferable you spend your time doing the important things that you love, instead of doing tasks which are unprofitable to you. As such, you should make it your goal to spend your time on tasks which you take joy in.

2. Beware of fads and trends. Trends are one big part of consumerism. So, to avoid the trouble altogether, it's best you avoid fads and trends. There's no point buying stuff for more because a popular name is written on it.

Day Twenty-Nine

1. It's likely that you're feeling stress right now as a result of many different factors such as work, family life, a busy schedule, or health issues. And a good percentage of our lives revolves around the use of technology. As such, even at the times when we should be de-stressing, technology takes a lot of our time. Minimalism revolves around limits. So, it's best you know when it's time to unplug from technologies such as devices and the internet and take a break.

2. The practical way of combating distractions and staying in tune with your goals for each day is to plan out your day. Draft a to-do list of what you hope to achieve each day. You will find that following it through will cut down on distractions.

Day Thirty

1. Build focus and discipline in your life by taking on practices that help you reduce the noise, distraction, and clutter in your life, such as meditation, yoga, mindfulness, etc. These practices are more productive and more valuable than other trivial activities like binge eating or watching TV. For a start, you can begin reducing the time you spend on

those trivial tasks and investing them in productive activities.

2. It is advisable you find a style that best fits you when practicing minimalism. Draft a routine for running your day, especially when you hit the hay and wake up. It helps you regulate your progress.

Conclusion

This book, ***Minimalist Budget: A Practical Guide To Start Minimalist Budget***, was written with these goals in mind: to spur you, the reader, into creating your own minimalist budget and, in doing so, becoming more financially secure. The chapters of this book have explored, extensively, what is meant by a minimalist budget and detailed out the way to go about writing one. But it also went beyond that. To ensure sustainability, subjects such as debt, financial principles, and decluttering were also dealt with.

Minimalism may seem daunting because many people know the word and talk about it, but only a few put the ideology into practice. It is my hope that this book has been successful at revealing what is truly meant by a minimalist lifestyle and budget. With that, I bid you godspeed on your journey to the achievement of your goals and financial freedom.

References

Amanda. (2017, June 2). Five reasons people never achieve minimalism. Retrieved from

https://thetinylife.com/five-reasons-people-never-achieve-minimalism/

Becker, J. (2010). When you are a minimalist but your partner isn't. Retrieved from

https://www.becomingminimalist.com/when-youre-a-minimalist-but-your-partner-isnt/

Becker, J. (2011). What is minimalism?. Retrieved from

https://www.becomingminimalist.com/what-is-minimalism/

Boyes, A. (2018, February 12). 6 benefits of an uncluttered mind. Retrieved from

https://www.google.com/amp/s/www.psychologytoday.com/us/blog/in-practice/201802/6-benefits-uncluttered-space%3famp

Gardner, B. (2015, May 16). Minimalism: a happier way to live. Retrieved from

https://www.google.com/amp/s/www.wanderlustworker.com/how-to-discipline-yourself-with-10-habits/amp/

Household spending, Canada, regions and provinces. Retrieved from https://www150.statcan.gc.ca/t1/tbl1/en/tv.action?pid=1110022201

Irby, L. (2019, May 14). Reasons debt is bad for you. Retrieved from

https://www.thebalance.com/reasons-debt-is-bad-960048

Jacobe, D. (2013, June 3). One in there Americans prepare a detailed household budget.

Retrieved from https://news.gallup.com/poll/162872/one-three-americans-prepare-detailed-household-budget.aspx

Job, V., Dweck, S. C., & Walton, G. M. (2010). Ego depletion-is it all in your head?

implicit theories about willpower affect self-regulation. *Psychological science, 21*, 1686-1693. Retrieved from https://doi.org/10.1177/0956797610384745

Kanaat, R. How to discipline yourself with 10 habits. Retrieved from

https://www.google.com/amp/s/www.wanderlustworker.com/how-to-discipline-yourself-with-10-habits/amp/

Kristen. (2019, March 18). How to create a minimalist budget. Retrieved from http://freshlyundone.com/how-to-create-minimalist-budget/

Leizrowice, R. (2017, February 12). How to fail at minimalism. Retrieved from

https://www.google.com/amp/s/www.rosieleizrowice.com/blog/howtofailatminimalism%3fformat=amp

Lustgarten, S. (2015, August 26). Minimalist budget: 5 ways to make it work. Retrieved

from https://nosidebar.com/minimalism-budget/

Michael, P. (2018, February 16). 7 warning signs you are in debt denial. Retrieved from

https://www.wisebread.com/7-warning-signs-youre-in-debt-denial

Millburn, J., & Nicodemus, R. What is minimalism?. Retrieved from

https://www.theminimalists.com/minimalism/

Nicodemus, R. & Millburn, F. J. (2015). A month of minimalism. Retrieved from

https://www.theminimalists.com/month/

Northwestern Mutual. (2018). Planning & Progress Study 2018. Retrieved from

https://news.northwesternmutual.com/planning-and-progress-2018

Ofei, M. (2018, February 5). What is minimalism? An introduction to living with intentionality. Retrieved from https://theminimalistvegan.com/what-is-minimalism/

Opperman, M. 10 warning signs of a debt problem. Retrieved from https://credit.org/2017/07/20/10-warning-signs-of-a-debt-problem/

Ramsey, D. (2009). The total money makeover. Nashville, TN: Thomas Nelson

Sun, L. (2017, November 20). A foolish take: here's how much debt the average U.S. household owes. Retrieved from https://www.usatoday.com/story/money/personalfinance/2017/11/18/a-foolish-take-heres-how-much-debt-the-average-us-household-owes/107651700/

The True Cost. (n.d.). Environmental Impact. Retrieved from https://truecostmovie.com/learn-more/environmental-impact/

Walker, M. [TED]. (2019, June 3). Sleep is your superpower. [Video file]. Retrieved from https://youtu.be/5MuIMqhT8DM

Why student loans are good. (2019, January 2). Retrieved from

https://www.debt.com/student-loan-debt/why-student-loans-are-good/amp/

www.ingramcontent.com/pod-product-compliance
Lightning Source LLC
Chambersburg PA
CBHW071349080526
44587CB00017B/3032